Editor
John Liebmann
Design
Peter Benoist
Picture Research
Jenny Golden
Production
Rosemary Bishop
Illustrations
Hayward Art Group
Endpaper map
Matthews and Taylor Associates
Author's assistant
Lucia Otto

First published 1980
Macdonald Educational Limited
Holywell House, Worship Street
London EC2A 2EN

© Macdonald Educational
Limited 1980

ISBN 0 356 06774 2 (cased edition)
ISBN 0 356 06775 0 (limp edition)

Made and printed by
Morrison & Gibb Limited
Edinburgh, Scotland

Colour reproduction by
Fotomecanica Iberico, Madrid

Photographic sources
Key to positions of illustrations:
(T) top, (C) centre, (B) bottom,
(L) left, (R) right.

*Agency for Public Information,
Jamaica:* 25(BR) *Allsport:* 47(R)
Mike Andrews: 42(TR) *BWIA:*
48–9 *Bo Bojesen:* 21(BL)
22(L), 25(TR), 28(B), 37(BL), 41(T),
47(BL) *Anne Bolt:* 8, 14–15, 16–17,
31, 38(L), 39(BR), 40(B), 43(BL,BR),
44(T), 44–45 *Camera Press:* 26(B),
30(B), 33(T), 35(BR) *Colorific:*
17(TR), 40(T) *Coconut Industry
Board:* 26(T) *Compix:* 19(TR), 20(T),
22(R), 27(B) *Embassy of Cuba:* 21(TR)
Explorer: 29(TL) *Peter Fraenkel:* 50
John Griffiths: 15(B), 23(TR,BL),
43(TL) *Susan Griggs:* 10, 28(T)
Robert Harding Associates: 2–3, 9(B),
21(BR), 25(TL), 33(BL), 34(B), 45(T),
47(TL) *Richard Hart:* 14(T) *Alan
Hutchison:* 6–7, 16(T), 17(BR),
33(BR), 36(BR), 38(B) *Jamaican
Tourist Board:* 34(T), 41(BR), 49(T)
William MacQuitty: 11(B), 29(B),
36(TL), 37(BR), 41(BL) *National
Maritime Museum:* 11(T) *Osiris Films:*
35(T) *Popperfoto:* 15(T) *Rex Features:*
13(B), 18, 24, 32, 51(TL), 50–51
Spectrum Colour Library:
9(TL), 19(BL), 20(BR), 25(BL),
39(T), 45(BR) *Homer Sykes:* 46,
49(B) *John Topham Picture Library:*
19(C) *Trinidad and Tobago High
Commission:* 29(TR) *Mireille Vautier:*
13(T), 35(BL), 39(BL) *David
Williams and Ketchum Limited:*
27(TR) *ZEFA:* 9(TR), 27(TL)
Caribbean Chronicle: 30(T), 48(L)
Tass from Sovfoto: 42
Abeng Group, Jamaica: 51(TR)

Endpaper: The outskirts of Kingston, Jamaica.
Page 6: Fishing off Carriacou, the largest of the Grenadines.
Cover picture shows field workers in Haiti, by Bo Bojesen.

The Caribbean

by
Ken Campbell

Macdonald Educational

Contents

Sea of contrasts

▲ The Caribbean islands lie in a line 3,000 kilometres long stretching from the United States to the north coast of Venezuela. They form a natural barrier between the Atlantic to the east and the Caribbean Sea which lies to the west.

Islands round a sea

The Caribbean Sea borders the east coast of Central and South America from Mexico to Venezuela. It is separated from the Gulf of Mexico in the north and the Atlantic in the east by a string of islands. The first people to live on these islands came many centuries ago from the mainland of South America. One group, called the Caribs, have given their name to the sea and hence to the islands which surround it – the Caribbean islands.

Apart from the name, very little remains of these first Caribbean people. The societies of the islands today have been shaped by the last 500 years of European and African influence.

The Caribbean islands are sometimes known as the West Indies. This is a reminder that the first Europeans to reach the Caribbean were looking for a westward route to India. They made their landfall in the Bahamas but believed they had already arrived in India, so they called the islands the Indies.

Though Europeans ruled the islands for several centuries, most of the people now living there are of African origin. Their ancestors were brought as slaves to work on the islands. Today Europeans, Africans and the few surviving Amerindians have been joined by Indians and Chinese. Each island has a particular racial mix which reflects its own individual history.

Independent states

Since Haiti became an independent state in 1804 the people on many of the other islands have followed suit. Each island has usually become a nation in its own right and the area has some of the smallest independent countries in the world. The only land border separating independent states lies between French-speaking Haiti and the Spanish-speaking Dominican Republic (not to be confused with the English-speaking island of Dominica to the south). The two countries share the island now called Hispaniola. Cuba, the largest island in the Caribbean, also has the largest population. At the other end of the scale some of the tiniest islands have a population measured in hundreds and remain linked to European countries. The large and industrialized island of Puerto Rico has become closely associated with the United States.

The climate and landscape has its contrasts too. Many of the smaller islands such as Anguilla or the Turks and Caicos Islands are quite flat and dry. The islands of the Greater Antilles group (Cuba, Jamaica, Hispaniola and Puerto Rico) are mountainous. The name Haiti actually means 'mountainous' in the language of its original inhabitants. Warm sunny weather is normal for much of the year but during the hurricane season this can change suddenly as fierce storms sweep across the area.

◀ An oil well off the coast of Trinidad. Oil has been produced in Trinidad since 1909 and has given the island a head-start in developing its own industries. As well as two oil refineries Trinidad has a petrochemical complex.

▲ Though most of the Caribbean islands now form part of independent states there are reminders everywhere of their colonial past. Devon House is Jamaica's national gallery, but was once an opulent private residence. In the former Spanish colonies there are fine cities dating back to the sixteenth century.

▼ In Cuba the government is developing new settlements in the countryside to stop the drift to overcrowded towns which is normal in the Caribbean. Cuba is a similar size to Great Britain though the population is much smaller. The language is Spanish and most Cubans are of Spanish or African descent.

▲ The peaceful town of St. Pierre and the active volcano Mt. Pelée which dominates the island of Martinique. Attractive beaches and wooded landscapes draw tourists to the Caribbean from Europe and North America. Martinique, like Guadeloupe, is administratively part of France.

Peopling of the Caribbean

The hurricane people

Early Caribbean settlers, such as the Taino-speaking Arawaks, Siboneys and Caribs, came from the American mainland. Many travelled from the area of the Orinoco River and were related to the people now commonly called Amerindians.

By the fifteenth century the Arawaks were living a settled farming life in the western Caribbean, growing cassava and sweet potatoes and fishing from dugout canoes. Arawak words such as 'hurricane' and 'barbecue' have passed into modern English.

The Caribs dominated the eastern Caribbean. They had a less advanced technology but their social organization was more suited to defence.

The newcomers

In 1492 a Spanish voyage of exploration led by Christopher Columbus opened up the Caribbean to Europe. Spain was followed by The Netherlands, France, England and Denmark in carving out parts of an empire. The colonizers came in search of gold and silver and demanded labour for their mines. Whole islands were depopulated by forced labour and disease. Any rebellions were savagely put down, as in the massacre of 1511 which followed the revolt of the Taino people in Puerto Rico.

Some wealthy Europeans made the Caribbean their home, although absentee landlords were common in the British colonies. A number of people also came from Europe to work under contract for the landowners. After completing their contract they often stayed behind to set up small farms of their own.

Into the unknown

In the seventeenth century large-scale sugar production began. This required a huge labour force. The plantation owners wanted to use the cheapest possible labour to do the work. It was eventually provided by enslavement of Africans. All the nations of western Africa from Senegal in the north to Angola in the south were raided for workers. Men and women were taken by force from their homes and families and shipped across the Atlantic to work as slaves on the Caribbean plantations.

Conditions on the Caribbean islands were exceptionally bad, even compared with other slave societies. More slaves were always needed to replace those who had been worked to death. A total of 750,000 slaves were taken to Jamaica but by the time the slaves were freed only 350,000 survived. In the Caribbean as a whole it is the descendants of these people taken by force from Africa into an unknown land who now form a majority of the population.

After Britain made trading in slaves illegal in 1807 other means had to be used to find labour. Indians and Chinese were persuaded to travel to the Caribbean to work under contract. Many of these indentured workers stayed behind after completing their contract. Trinidad especially relied on an Asian workforce because sugar production was not developed there until the nineteenth century. This can be seen in the large Asian population of Trinidad today.

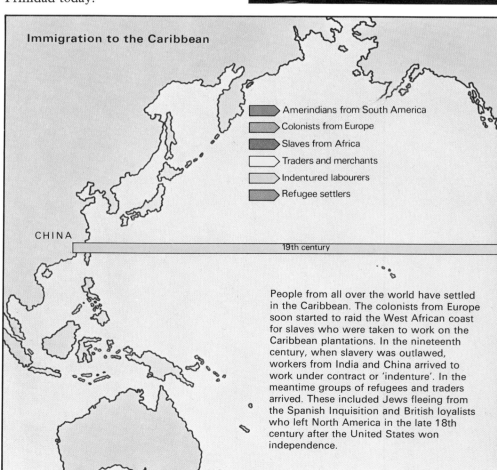

Immigration to the Caribbean

- Amerindians from South America
- Colonists from Europe
- Slaves from Africa
- Traders and merchants
- Indentured labourers
- Refugee settlers

CHINA

19th century

People from all over the world have settled in the Caribbean. The colonists from Europe soon started to raid the West African coast for slaves who were taken to work on the Caribbean plantations. In the nineteenth century, when slavery was outlawed, workers from India and China arrived to work under contract or 'indenture'. In the meantime groups of refugees and traders arrived. These included Jews fleeing from the Spanish Inquisition and British loyalists who left North America in the late 18th century after the United States won independence.

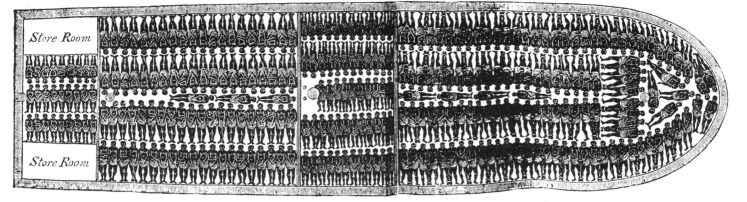

▲ The European ships which carried captured Africans across the Atlantic were designed to cram as many people as possible in the space below decks. Many of the captives died on the journey. Those who survived were sold as slaves.

◄ The cathedral at Santo Domingo, capital of the Dominican Republic, houses the tomb of Christopher Columbus. In his four voyages of exploration Columbus visited and re-named most of the Caribbean islands.

◄ The island of Aruba where descendants of the original Amerindian inhabitants survived to inter-marry with later European and African immigrants. On most of the other Caribbean islands the Arawaks, Caribs and other Amerindian people were wiped out during the early centuries of European rule. A few Caribs survived on Dominica.

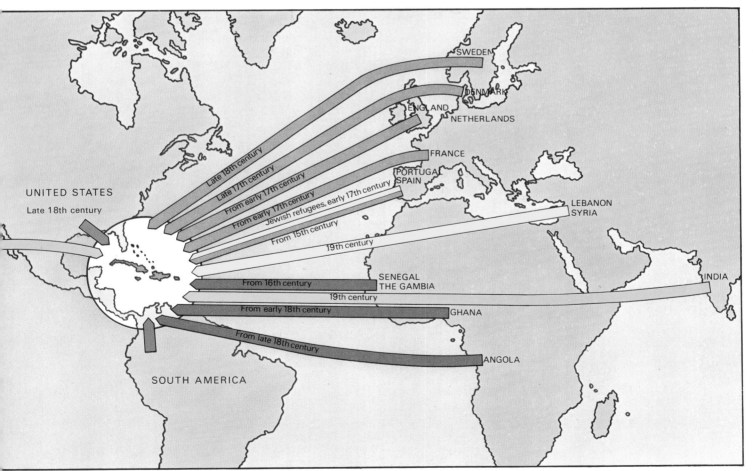

Resistant Africa

Human dignity denied

Slavery was like a prison sentence passed on a whole people. Once in the Caribbean, the slaves were stripped of all dignity by their owners, who used them just as work-machines. They received no pay, and were given only the food, clothing and shelter needed to keep them working.

Slaves were forbidden to practise their religion, speak their own language or even live with their families. It was a life without comfort. Yet the slaves fought back and survived. Every trace of African culture in the Caribbean today is a reminder of their resistance.

Freedom fighters

Many slaves chose death rather than slavery. In Cuba there were mass suicides. Some slaves mutilated themselves so that their owners could not get as much work from them. Women tried to make sure they had as few children as possible, rather than see them born into servitude.

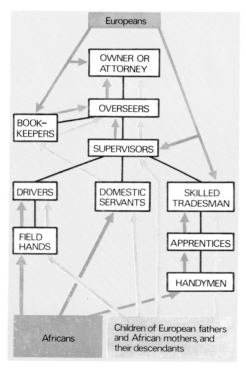

▲ The social structure of a Caribbean plantation. Europeans were in charge while Africans did the menial work. Even after slavery was abolished the pattern did not change very much, and was even repeated in colonies which had no plantations.

From the beginning slaves ran away. Many were quickly recaptured and maimed, tortured or murdered by their masters. But in spite of being in a strange land, others managed to survive in groups. The runaways were called Maroons. They set up fortified states, especially in mountain areas. The British fought two wars against the Maroons in Jamaica in the eighteenth century. The Maroons were not defeated, so the British negotiated treaties with them and left them alone. In Dominica in 1785 an alliance of Caribs and Maroons put a price of £100 on the governor's head.

A free republic

Throughout the whole slave period revolts erupted from Barbados to the Virgin Islands and Guadeloupe to Trinidad. The greatest of all saw half a million slaves in the French colony of St. Domingue rise up and establish the free republic of Haiti in 1804. This encouraged Black freedom-fighters everywhere but made many slave-owners even more brutal for fear of similar rebellions.

The slave system survived because of the huge profits it brought to the plantation owners. Jamaica's crop in 1805 was worth £5 million in sugar and rum. The slaves received none of this although it all came through their hard work. Even when slaves in the British Empire were freed in 1838 they received no compensation for loss of their country, family and liberty. Instead the British government paid £20 million to their owners.

In the Morant Bay rebellion of 1865 Jamaican ex-slaves and their descendants protested against their intolerable living conditions. The lack of land available for settlement was one of their grievances. Fearing a repetition of events in Haiti, the British governor put down the revolt with great savagery. Nearly 600 people were executed, 600 more were flogged and 1,000 homes were destroyed.

African roots

Since the slaves came from different parts of Africa they did not all speak the same language. To prevent them speaking to each other and plotting rebellion, the owners often deliberately bought slaves who spoke different languages. The owners did not bother to learn their slaves' languages – the slaves had to learn to take orders in English, French or Spanish.

▲ A statue of Paul Bogle, leader of the Morant Bay rebellion. In the reprisals which followed, Bogle was executed by the colonial authorities.

▼ Jamaican names and their equivalent in the Fanti language of Ghana. Slaves were forbidden to use their own names and had to take a nickname or the name of their master. Some people nevertheless managed to preserve the old names and today they are becoming more popular again.

Jamaican name	Fanti name
Cubina	Kobina
Quaco	Kweku
Cuffee Cophy Coffee	Kofi
Quamina Quamin	Kwamina

From this the Creole languages were born. The slaves began to use European words to talk to each other, and soon a new language developed which used many European words but had a grammatical structure which was familiar to its African speakers. Creole soon became the natural language among the slaves, and later generations learnt it as their first language.

Today the Caribbean is uncovering its African roots. There is a new pride in the Creoles as true Caribbean languages, which can take their place alongside the 'official' English and French of the islands.

▲ A painting in the Haitian style showing Toussaint L'Ouverture, who is celebrated throughout the Caribbean as well as in his native Haiti. Following the slave uprising of 1791 Toussaint led the takeover of the French colony of St. Domingue and successfully repulsed a British invasion from Jamaica. In 1802 Napoleon Bonaparte's soldiers attempted to restore French control over St. Domingue. They captured Toussaint and he died in a French prison, but his success as a revolutionary is commemorated in his name L'Ouverture, which means 'the opener'. Unlike Guadeloupe and Martinique, St. Domingue successfully resisted Napoleon. In 1804 Toussaint's successor Dessalines triumphantly proclaimed it to be the free Black republic of Haiti.

▶ Black consciousness lives on in the Caribbean. This Black Power march in Trinidad in 1970 was part of a wave of protest through-out the Caribbean sparked off by the arrest of Caribbean students in Canada. In Trinidad these broadened into a national upsurge with wide popular backing.

13

The national movement

First steps

Emancipation gave slaves freedom, but not necessarily justice. They were still subordinate to the landowners and merchants who made up the colonial parliaments and governments. Only those people who had a certain amount of land were allowed to vote. Because the former slaves had no land they had no vote either.

There was no Caribbean nationalism until the many groups of people who had been brought into each island began to think of it as their home. In 1804 Haiti became the first self-governing Caribbean nation. It was promptly isolated by the European powers who still controlled all the other islands in the area. France demanded huge payments in compensation for the profitable investments that it lost. Together these actions crippled Haiti from birth, and it is now one of the poorest countries in the world. But it is still respected by Caribbean people for having achieved

▲ The Caribbean Labour Congress (CLC) held its founding meeting in Barbados in 1945. Because the majority of the people had no political rights trade union bodies were an important means for expressing national aspirations. The CLC was a Caribbean-wide organization which worked for an independent federation of the colonies. It broke up at the height of the Cold War, but in its short life it had a formidable impact. A number of prominent national figures can be identified here: T.A. Marryshow of Grenada, first president of the CLC (middle row, fifth from right); Grantley Adams, later Prime Minister of Barbados (middle row, fourth from right); Vere Bird, later Prime Minister of Antigua (back row, third from right).

◄ Tubal Uriah 'Buzz' Butler was born in 1897 in Grenada. Like many Grenadians he worked in the Trinidad oilfields where he organized strikes and hunger marches. After he was arrested, copies of this photograph were circulated among fellow workers who collected money to help with his defence. Butler was one of the first Trinidadian leaders to unite people of Asian and African origin. He later became an active parliamentarian and died in 1977.

▶ The Red House, home of Trinidad's parliament. Today all adults may vote, but at first the parliament only represented the small minority who owned land. Until 1944, 95% of the people of Britain's Caribbean colonies had no vote.

freedom against all the odds. The eastern part of the island of Hispaniola passed briefly into French hands, then back under Spanish control. It achieved independence as the Dominican Republic in 1844.

In the nineteenth century Cuba and Puerto Rico forced Spain to relinquish the rest of its Caribbean empire. Those settlers who wanted freedom from Spanish control joined forces with slaves and free blacks to fight for independence. C. M. de Cespedes freed the slaves from his sugar plantation in 1868 and declared Cuba independent. By 1897 Puerto Rico had won autonomy from Spain and Cuba was winning its liberation war.

Independence

In the British empire the struggle began with the protest of ordinary workers against unjust living conditions. They had few trade unions, no political parties and rarely even a vote. They nevertheless protested through strikes and demonstrations. These swept through the British Caribbean, beginning from St. Kitts in 1935. Their impact was so strong that some members of the middle class such as lawyers, doctors and civil servants

joined in on their side. The Caribbean community overseas also played a prominent role in the political struggle.

In the years since the Second World War Jamaica, Trinidad, Barbados, The Bahamas, Grenada, Dominica, St. Lucia, and St. Vincent and the Grenadines have achieved independence.

Closer association

Independence can bring its problems, and many people argue that prosperity can come only by close association with a richer and more powerful country. These ideas won out in 1952 in Puerto Rico when it became a commonwealth associated with the United States. Puerto Ricans are American citizens, although they do not have a vote in US elections. The French islands of Guadeloupe and Martinique became overseas *départements* of France in 1846. The Netherlands Antilles have adopted an intermediate position. They have a parliament of their own, but remain associated with the Netherlands. Most of the former British colonies have passed through this stage on the way to complete independence. Anguilla, Antigua and St. Kitts-Nevis are still associated with Britain.

▼ In 1961 a group of Cuban exiles, who were opposed to the new communist-led government, invaded the island at the Bay of Pigs. It was later disclosed that they were financed and supported by the Central Intelligence Agency of the United States. This Cuban poster commemorates their defeat at Playa Giron, and emphasizes Cuba's opposition to United States influence.

▼ Luis Munoz Marin became the first elected governor of Puerto Rico in 1948. He is seen here (right) with President Truman of the United States. Marin annexed his country to the US in the hope that American investment would help it to prosper. But his Puerto Rican model for economic development of Third World countries has not solved the country's crucial problem of unemployment, which stood at 21.3% in 1976.

Colonial vestiges

Spoils of war

Colonization of the Caribbean began in 1494 with a Spanish settlement in Santo Domingo. Soon all the European imperial powers were fighting over the rich sugar islands. St. Lucia changed hands 14 times between Britain and France.

Some colonies were actually put up for sale. Sweden bought St. Barthélémy from the French in 1785, and in 1917 the US paid Denmark 25 million dollars for three of the Virgin Islands. Certain small islands, like Mustique in the Grenadines, have even been sold to individuals as private property.

Many colonies have proved valuable for their strategic position. The British settled in Bermuda in 1612 and used it as the base for their West Indies forces. It is still a colony and the site of military bases linked to NATO. The US established a naval base at Guantanamo in Cuba in 1902, and has kept it ever since.

Outposts of Empire

The inhabitants of the British colonies were always encouraged to think of Britain as the 'Motherland'. They were as welcome to go to Britain as Britons were to settle in the Caribbean. They were all British subjects.

The French system went further. Its colonies elected representatives to sit in parliament in Paris. In 1946 Martinique and Guadeloupe became classified as overseas *départements*, or counties, of France. They are ruled just as if they were part of France itself, not thousands of miles away in the Caribbean. They elect three representatives to the National Assembly and two Senators.

The Dutch Antilles rule themselves to a greater extent than this. But they have no control over their foreign affairs and defence which are determined in the Netherlands.

Since 1917 Puerto Ricans have had US citizenship, but their language,

culture and history set them apart from their fellow citizens. There have been attempts to change the language in the schools on the island from Spanish to English, but the Puerto Ricans successfully resisted them.

Looking to the future

Although most people in the Caribbean now live in independent states, they face a future marked by five centuries of colonization. The boundaries of the states were made by the colonists, and they do not always make geographical sense. The Bahamas are separated from the neighbouring Turks and Caicos Islands, and the tiny island of St. Martin is divided between France and the Netherlands.

The European languages are another legacy from the colonial era. English, French, Spanish and Dutch are still the only official languages used in the Caribbean.

The main problem now is that the economies of the former colonies are still strongly influenced by the needs of their old masters. The Caribbean nations are still working for economic as well as political independence.

'*All peoples have an inalienable right to complete freedom, the exercise of their sovereignty and the integrity of their national territory.*'

▲ Part of the resolution on colonialism adopted by the United Nations in 1960. The world-wide mood of opposition to colonialism encouraged colonies in the Caribbean in their quest for independence.

◄ Rural scene in Martinique, which has the status of an overseas *département* of France.

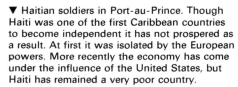

▼ Banks galore in the Cayman Islands. Though still linked to Britain, the Cayman Islands have their own tax laws which encourage banks based overseas to do business from the islands. This brings some immediate prosperity, but does not hold out any long-term hope for independence.

▲ Main street of Charlotte Amalie, St. Thomas, capital of the United States Virgin Islands. The mail box, the stars and stripes, and the strolling tourists show the influence of the United States today on these small islands. The architecture dates from the period of Danish rule which lasted until 1917.

▼ Haitian soldiers in Port-au-Prince. Though Haiti was one of the first Caribbean countries to become independent it has not prospered as a result. At first it was isolated by the European powers. More recently the economy has come under the influence of the United States, but Haiti has remained a very poor country.

The natural environment

Geological diversity

Puerto Rico, Jamaica, Cuba, and the island of Hispaniola are formed from fold mountains. Most of Haiti is mountainous, and the range stretches into the Dominican Republic where it rises to over 3,000 metres. In the eastern Caribbean two quite different geological forms predominate. The inner islands from Saba to Grenada are of volcanic origin, and there are active volcanoes on a number of them.

Soufrière on St. Vincent continually pours volcanic ash on to the surrounding countryside. On Montserrat even the sand is volcanic and it is black. Like the mountainous Greater Antilles, these islands tend to have high rainfall. Dominica is famous for its virgin rain-forest and is said to have a river for every day of the year.

The Virgin Islands, Anguilla, Antigua and Barbados are composed of limestone and coral. They are relatively low-lying and tend to be drier. Consequently they have few rivers. The butterfly-shaped island of Guadeloupe has both geological types. The eastern part, called Grande Terre, is of low-lying limestone. It is separated by a salt-water river from the western island which includes an active volcano, also called Soufrière.

Tropical and temperate

The Caribbean climate accommodates both tropical and temperate plants and is a botanist's paradise. The beauties of the environment can be practical as well as attractive. The gourds from the calabash tree make a useful drinking vessel, and annatto will colour a stew bright orange. The famous St. Vincent botanical gardens were laid out in 1763. The breadfruit tree, which is native to the South Pacific, was taken first to St. Vincent. Today breadfruit is a common food throughout the Caribbean. Mahogany from the Dominican Republic is a popular

▲ This scene of destruction in Roseau, Dominica, shows the damage caused by Hurricane David in late August 1979. In just a few hours three-quarters of the population of Dominica lost their homes as roofs were ripped off and walls were demolished. The hurricane moved away north-westwards, and a few days later several hundred people were killed when it devastated parts of the Dominican Republic. Crops were destroyed too. Hurricane David flattened most of the banana plantations on which Dominica depends for its income.

▶ The hurricane season lasts from June to November each year. Every year there are several storms which develop out in the Atlantic and gain strength as they move westwards. Winds of up to 300 km/h are accompanied by torrential rain. Flood damage is often as severe as the destruction caused by the wind itself. Two typical hurricane pathways are shown here. After crossing the Caribbean Hurricane Charlie of 1951 continued westwards towards Central America. Others, like David, take a more northerly course and eventually hit Florida, Louisiana or Texas. Only the very south of the Caribbean is safe from hurricanes.

hardwood used for furniture making. The Bermuda cedar produced another sought-after timber until it was blighted by disease.

Wildlife is equally varied. There are huge colonies of flamingoes in the Bahamas and Bonaire. The manatee is an unusual sea mammal found only in the Caribbean and in South American rivers which flow into the Atlantic. The turtle is another noted sea-dweller. It has been hunted almost to extinction for its skin and flesh, but there is now a turtle farm in the Cayman Islands which aims to replenish stocks.

Another animal unique to the area is the mountain chicken of Dominica and Montserrat. Despite its name it is not a fowl but a giant frog.

Though the climate is often ideal, nature has its revenge from time to time. Hurricanes, earthquakes and volcanic eruptions have all taken their toll. Trinidad, Margarita, Aruba, Bonaire and Curaçao are outside the hurricane zone, but all the other islands from Tobago northwards are at risk. Kingston, Jamaica was all but destroyed by a fire which followed the earthquake of 1907.

▲ A flock of scarlet ibis taking off. This spectacular bird is one of Trinidad's tourist attractions. There is a large ibis colony on Caroni Swamp, just south of Port of Spain. Other colourful birds also inhabit the area. Trinidad's Carib name was Iere, which means 'land of the humming bird'.

◄ The beach at Charlotteville, Tobago. Scenes like this are a precious economic asset for the Caribbean. Tourists from Europe and North America come to enjoy the warm sea, sunshine and unspoilt beaches fringed with palm trees. Great care is needed to ensure that the hotels and tourist facilities which are springing up do not damage the environment for future generations.

Working in the Caribbean

From machete to machine

In the past the greatest contributors to the economies of the Caribbean islands were the sugar workers. They are typified by the cane cutter wielding a machete. There is still a great deal of manual work to be done in the sugar fields, though machines are slowly replacing people on the bigger estates.

In one form or another, agriculture remains a major activity throughout the region. Though tourism is now the main source of foreign exchange for St. Lucia, over 50% of the island's workforce are employed in the banana industry.

Patterns of employment

There is no single pattern of work which applies to the whole region. This is partly due to traditional differences in land policy. In many islands small farms abound. They were first set up by freed slaves who moved away from the plantations. But in Barbados, for example, land was made expensive to buy so that people were forced to remain at work on the plantations.

Throughout the area many people still work on the big estates. The enormous Rio Haina plantation in the Dominican Republic has over 25,000 hectares of sugar cane – more than the total area of sugar in Barbados. By contrast, agriculture in Grenada has concentrated on cocoa and spices and this has led to a number of small and medium-sized farms. Thousands of people provide food for themselves by fishing from the sea but there is still not very much large-scale fishing in the area, except in Cuba.

Women make up a substantial part of the workforce everywhere even

▲ Dockers on the way to work at Bridgetown, Barbados. Good port facilities are essential for trade between the islands and further afield. The deep-water harbour at Bridgetown was opened in 1961. Ports are now being modernized to deal with container traffic. The container system was first used on the Puerto Rico–US route.

▶ A small farm in Cave Valley, Jamaica. Well over 90% of Jamaica's farms are smallholdings, though they occupy less than half the available agricultural land. Food crops of all sorts are grown. The smallholders also cultivate sugar cane. Although they often produce a surplus of food to sell, the smallholdings are often not big enough to support a whole family. Many members of rural families have to take paid jobs to supplement their income from the land. By contrast Haiti has a true peasant economy in which most people live directly off small agricultural plots.

though child-care facilities are usually very poor. Often a grandmother or other relative looks after the children while the parents are at work. Trade unions are well established in the larger industries, as with the Oilfield Workers Trade Union of Trinidad and Tobago. Through the unions, workers try to ensure that their pay and conditions are satisfactory. The large oil refineries of Curaçao and Bonaire have attracted workers from all over the Caribbean.

Servicing the system

The governments everywhere are large employers. During the period 1969–73 the number of public-service workers in Puerto Rico increased by 50%. Professional salaries and those of public employees compare well with European standards although they do not approach United States levels.

Employment is also provided by international interests. 'Off-shore' banking, which benefits from generous tax laws, sustains the Cayman Islands. Barbados has recently introduced new laws which give tax advantages to international companies. Similar tax-havens already exist in Bermuda and the Bahamas where company name plates virtually obscure the façades of some buildings.

▲ The crew working on the deck of one of Cuba's large modern fishing vessels. As well as working close to home the Cuban fleet fishes in the distant waters of the North Atlantic or off the Canary Islands. The crews on the distant-water trawlers work a continuous duty which may be many months long. They are then flown home for an equal period of paid holiday. The trawlers are serviced by large depot ships which bring supplies, exchange crews and collect the catch.

▼ A co-operative meeting. Jamaica has a well-developed co-operative movement. Instead of selling their produce individually, small farmers combine to get a better price. The movement has also developed co-operative farms and even co-operative banks or credit unions.

▲ A sugar-cane cutter at work in St. Lucia. Perhaps more than any other job, cutting cane symbolizes work in the Caribbean. Until the arrival of modern machinery the cane cutter's long machete was the only means of gathering in the sugar crop which provides the mainstay of the economy of many islands. In many places competitions are held to find the champion cane cutter of the island or district. Like work in the sugar factories, cane cutting can only take place at certain times of the year.

Education for living

Towards the total school

In the Caribbean education is seen as too important a matter to be left only to the schools. It will be many years before there are enough schools and teachers for everyone. In Jamaica a shift system is in operation. Each school has a morning and an afternoon shift, making education available to double the number of students. In Haiti only one child in ten gets a chance to go to school.

The shortage of facilities is aggravated by the youthfulness of the Caribbean's population. In Barbados, for instance, half the people are less than 20 years old. Nevertheless Barbados has an excellent record of primary education and has begun to provide for pre-school children. Overall though, nursery education is the exception and Grandma remains a strong influence as child-minder and first teacher.

Education is being treated more and more as a life-long process which takes place in and out of the classroom. In Cuba all schools now mix periods of study with periods of work. Elsewhere civic responsibility, agriculture, health and family care have been given equal status with traditional subjects.

The media as teacher

Radio is by far the most popular source of news and entertainment. Most countries have more than one station, whether commercial or public. The Dominican Republic has 70. There are also a number of television channels showing imported and local programmes. The Jamaican government has recognized that it is wasteful for a poor country not to use the media for educational ends. The Jamaica Movement for the Advancement of Adult Learning (JAMAL) produces educational programmes which are mixed into the regular schedule. They enable people to learn history, geography and mathematics in an enjoyable and undemanding way.

Inadequate education in the past means that most of the islands have had to confront a high illiteracy rate, especially among the older generation. The local press now provides simplified news items for people who have just learned to read, and publicizes details of literacy events taking place around the country.

▼ A class in session in one of Jamaica's basic schools, which prepare children for primary school. The government provides teachers and pays the running costs but each community has to provide the buildings for its own basic school. Basic-school teachers are not usually fully qualified and receive in-service training. Jamaica's education policy guarantees education up to 17 years of age. This is followed by two years of compulsory service in hospitals, on farms or in the construction industry, or as a sports coach, assistant teacher or teacher in a basic school. Higher education then follows for those who qualify.

▼ Students at a St. Vincent secondary school studying chemistry. In the Commonwealth Caribbean education follows the British pattern and students who wish to go on to higher education must first complete their O- and A-levels. Until recently the exams themselves were set in Britain, but since 1979 the Caribbean Examination Council has provided exams to its own syllabus tailored to meet local needs.

The system inherited

In the colonial period schools were of a very high standard but only a small élite group attended them. Advanced education, similar to that of British public schools, was provided at places like Jamaica College, Codrington College in Barbados, and Queens Royal College in Trinidad. Students could then continue to university in Britain. There were old-established Spanish-speaking universities in the Caribbean at Santo Domingo (founded 1538) and Havana (founded 1728).

In response to the demand for education the colleges have been opened to everyone on the basis of merit. In the past the town schools received more than their fair share of resources, leaving many rural schools with poor buildings and facilities. To reverse the drift to the urban areas the Jamaican government has recently created special sports schools in the countryside.

▲ Students at a Cuban farm school taking care of cleaning and maintenance. In Cuba many secondary schools are built in the countryside and have farm areas attached. The pupils are responsible for agricultural work as well as their academic studies. The Sandino Citrus Fruit enterprise in western Cuba is an example of this mixture of education and production. It has 10,000 hectares of citrus on which most of the work is done by the 15,000 students from a number of schools around the estate.

▼ An adult literacy class in Cuba. Many of today's adults only had a very poor school education and some had none at all. Teaching reading and writing has therefore been a high priority in the Caribbean.

▲ The first newspaper in the Caribbean was the *Weekly Jamaican Current* which began publication in 1718. Bermuda's *Royal Gazette*, founded in 1828, is the oldest surviving title. The press and broadcasting play an important part in supplementing formal adult education.

Making the most of leisure

Time off

During the slave years the mass of labourers had hardly any leisure. The African slaves were not even allowed to celebrate their traditional festivals. Holidays were sometimes granted for the Christian celebrations at Easter and Christmas or for 'crop-over' at the end of harvest time. Religious festivals are still occasions for holidays. In the carnival islands preparations for the annual event take up a great deal of time in the weeks before Lent. Costumes have to be designed and sewn, songs composed and music learned. It is like belonging to a gigantic amateur dramatic society.

Board games are popular all the year round, but in Jamaica it is dominoes which is played most of all. A game can be set up in a moment as long as someone has a set of domino pieces. Like card games, dominoes is a social pastime at which people relax and chat. Domino tournaments are often organized in clubs, at home or even out of doors.

Children spend much of their time in the open enjoying the ideal climate of sun tempered by sea breezes. Marbles is a favourite game. The singing of ring-games can be heard everywhere. One of these simple tunes 'Brown Girl in the Ring' became a hit record in Europe for Boney M.

Sun and sea

Other people's free time provides the Caribbean with a thriving industry. The plantation great houses played host to visitors from Europe so that their owners could keep in touch with European styles. Later the warm climate and fine beaches of the area began to attract people rich enough to make the long sea journey.

Bermuda was among the first islands to encourage tourism. Although it lies outside the tropical zone and the Caribbean Sea it is warmed by the Gulf Stream current. Its winters are mild and it attracts people from the eastern United States who seek respite from their cold winters. In Jamaica tourism started as a government enterprise in 1888 with the construction of the 100-room Constant Spring Hotel. Nowadays improved communications and reduced working hours in the industrialized countries mean that tourism is no longer only for the very rich. Many ordinary people from Europe, North America and the USSR are now able to enjoy a holiday in the Caribbean sunshine.

A new industry

Caribbean-wide co-operation has turned tourism into a sophisticated industry. Careful planning is needed to ensure that food and entertainment can be provided from local resources and are not simply imported. Barbados is the site of the Caribbean Tourist Research Centre which analyses the regional development of tourism. Bermuda has an advanced School of Hotel Technology in Bermuda College. The Bahamas Hotel Training Council attracts students from all over the world.

One relative newcomer is St. Lucia. It started to encourage big-time tourism in the 1960s and its first luxury hotel was built in 1966. Within ten years tourism grew to rival the long-established banana industry in importance.

The high season for tourism is in the northern hemisphere's winter. Fewer foreign tourists come in summer. The citizens of Cuba and Jamaica are being encouraged by their governments to take holidays at this time of year and make use of the tourist facilities of their own country. People who have emigrated from the Caribbean are also tempted to 'come home' with their friends for holidays.

The tourist industry provides employment in services, construction and food production. As a spin-off from tourism some of the smaller islands have been equipped with a modern airport and sophisticated telecommunications.

▼ Leisurely horse-drawn surreys are a tourist attraction at Nassau, capital of the Bahamas. The tourist industry is central to the Bahamian economy. It provides jobs for two-thirds of the island's working population and brings in hundreds of millions of dollars every year. Most Bahamians live on New Providence but tourist developments are now springing up on more of the outlying islands of the group.

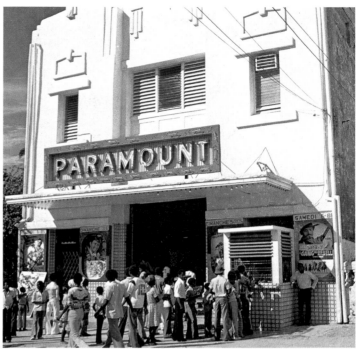

▲ Dunns River Falls are a traditional leisure attraction for Jamaicans on weekend outings and on holiday. In recent years foreign tourists have joined the local visitors. The hotels and facilities built for foreign tourists are used increasingly by local people in the off-season.

▼ A domino match under way in Jamaica. Board games such as chess, draughts, Chinese checkers and ludo are popular throughout the Caribbean but in Jamaica dominoes beats them all. The game is taken seriously and can generate excitement even among the spectators.

▲ The cinema is a great attraction throughout the Caribbean. Some are open-air, some are drive-in and many are large. This small local cinema in Haiti still manages to draw the crowds. Like cinemas the world over it has the next week's programmes advertised outside.

▲ The British liner Queen Elizabeth II at anchor off Martinique. Like many other liners the QE2 is used on cruises round the Caribbean, stopping off for a day or two at each island. The cruise ships bring tourists to the area from Europe, North America and further afield. The ships act as floating hotels for their passengers. This form of tourism does not bring as much economic benefit to the Caribbean as the residential tourists who patronize local hotels.

Agriculture for export

► Coconut palms growing on an experimental plantation in Jamaica. Coconuts are grown commercially throughout the Caribbean and form the basis for a number of industries. The oil is used for cooking and in soap manufacture. Coir fibre, which is obtained from the husk, is used to make matting and as a filling for mattresses and upholstery. The nut itself provides coconut milk as well as the soft white flesh which is used in cooking and confectionery.

▼ Curing tobacco in Cuba. The leaves are carefully dried to produce the material which is smoked. Tobacco is a native crop but its importance fell with the coming of sugar. Small farmers survived mainly in Cuba, Jamaica and Puerto Rico. Cuba's famous hand-rolled Havana cigars are possibly the best in the world.

A vast enterprise

The settlers from Europe who colonized the Caribbean turned the area into a huge agricultural enterprise, broken up only by sea and mountains. The entire activity was geared to providing food for consumption in Europe. Later it provided raw materials for European factories. This pattern still exists to a considerable extent. For example, Grenada's cocoa is exported to Britain and re-imported as expensive chocolate bars.

By the eighteenth century 'King Sugar' was the undisputed ruler and vast plantations met European demand. Sugar cane must be crushed immediately after it is cut, otherwise the raw juice loses some of its sweetness. Sugar mills were built on the plantations to produce the juice for export. Today there are a number of factories in the area making refined sugar, although much refining is still done abroad.

Rum

Barbados was the first to discover the delights of 'rumbullion', obtained by fermenting sugar juice from the vats. Today rum is produced on almost every island. Many islands have their own internationally famous brands. When liquor was banned in the United States during the Prohibition era of the 1920s and 1930s, Cuba, Bermuda and the Bahamas were sources of illegal supplies.

The main by-product of sugar is bagasse, the residue which is left after the juice has been crushed out. Bagasse is used for fuel and animal feed and for making hardboard. Cuba has a research institute devoted to the uses of sugar by-products.

Spice islands

Grenada is a real spice island, with nutmeg and mace as two of its most important exports. Both these spices come from the same tree and are separated and graded before shipment. They are so important to Grenada that a nutmeg appears on its national flag. Jamaica exports ginger and the allspice or pimento.

Citrus fruits, especially oranges and grapefruit, are exported fresh or canned. Dominica provides limes for a well-known brand of lime juice. A high-quality cotton known as sea island cotton is grown in the eastern Caribbean islands, especially Montserrat. It is marketed by the West Indies Sea Island Cotton Association, and many fine cotton garments made in Britain bear the WISCA mark on the label. Cotton is also grown in Cuba. Puerto Rico, Cuba and Jamaica have substantial textile industries.

Cattle ranching is big business in the Dominican Republic and Cuba. It is developing elsewhere, especially on the drier low-lying islands such as Barbados and Antigua. Poultry rearing is carried out successfully in many islands and provides an important source of protein.

▲ The Jamaican liqueur Tia Maria combines the flavour of Blue Mountain coffee with the kick of rum. Several other flavours including chocolate, coconut and pineapple provide the basis for a range of Caribbean drinks. Curaçao liqueur is made from oranges in the island of the same name. The formula for Trinidad's unique Angostura bitters is so secret that it is kept locked in a bank vault.

▲ Packing bananas in Martinique. The fruit can deteriorate rapidly and must be kept cool in transit. For this reason large-scale cultivation for export did not begin until the twentieth century when refrigerated ships became available. Bananas are easily bruised and have to be carefully boxed and sprayed with a protective coating before shipment. The banana plant can grow six metres tall or more. Though it looks like a tree the 'trunk' is really made up of the stems of its huge leaves. A mature banana plant produces fruit for at least 20 years but hurricane damage may destroy it prematurely. In St. Lucia dwarf strains of banana are being interplanted with coconut palms to give some protection from storms.

▶ Arrowroot fields in St. Vincent with an old processing factory in the background. The arrowroot plant is native to the area. Its thick underground stem is the source of a particularly pure form of starch used for medicinal purposes and in invalid and baby food. St. Vincent is one of the world's leading producers of arrowroot, which forms one of the island's most important exports.

Houses and homes

Town and country

There is no single lifestyle which is characteristic of the entire Caribbean area. Even within a single island there are tremendous differences, especially between town and country.

When the slaves were freed by their owners most people stayed behind on the same plantations and worked for a wage. But a few people were given land where they could set up small farms of their own. Others had to find space in the poorer lands in order to eke out a living. Many of the small farms which were set up then still exist today as family plots of land. They often provide a stable element in family life and a true home. Children sometimes live on the farm with their grandmother or aunt while their parents are elsewhere finding work.

In order to get work many people have moved from the country into the towns and cities. There has been a serious shortage of housing in the cities. As a result terrible slums have sprung up as people have had to build themselves what shelter they could out of wood or corrugated iron.

Family life

In many Caribbean communities children are brought up by their mother alone, or by members of the extended family such as their grandmother or aunt. In the days of slavery it was impossible for a man to look after his own children. Today the need to move away to find work means that fathers, and sometimes mothers too, must live away from their children.

Marriage is quite uncommon in some communities, at least among young people. People sometimes marry in later life – maybe after their children have grown up. It is often only at that stage that people are able to set up a home of their own, away from their own parents and immediate family.

In other sections of society the nuclear family is more common. Here children live together with both their parents. This system is usual in the wealthier farming areas and among professional people in the towns, for example. In Cuba the Family Code defines the domestic responsibilities of husbands as well as wives, and forms part of the marriage ceremony.

A fusion of styles

Many African and European nations have converged in the Caribbean and consequently a variety of building styles can be seen. The different traditions of the people are further modified by the restricted range of building materials to be found on each island.

In places where wood is plentiful it has naturally been used as a building material. Corrugated iron is a cheap and popular material for roofs. Wooden houses can be very comfortable and elegant but they do not stand up well to storms and earthquakes. Brick, concrete and glass are now much more widely used as new blocks of offices and flats spring up. Guadeloupe has a number of blocks of flats in the French style. Jamaica and Cuba are building multi-storey blocks in their efforts to improve housing conditions.

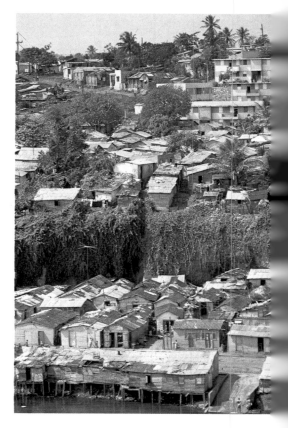

▲ A poor district of Santo Domingo, capital of the Dominican Republic. People who have crowded into the towns in search of work have had to find shelter in small, makeshift dwellings like those in the foreground near the water. Many of the big cities in the Caribbean have shanty town districts consisting entirely of houses like this. Shanty towns usually lack even the most basic services such as running water or a sewerage system. Better-quality housing, such as can be seen in the background, is being built as fast as possible.

▼ Mealtime outdoors in Haiti. The warm climate of the Caribbean allows much of life to be lived out of doors. Trailing vines, bougainvillea or christophene provide much-needed shade from the sun. Most Caribbean houses are single-storey bungalows. Often they are fitted with shutters to provide some protection against hurricanes. Multi-storey blocks of flats are common in Guadeloupe and Martinique. Cuba and Jamaica are also turning to this form of housing as a way of providing new homes quickly.

◀ A small farmstead in St. Vincent. Most town-dwellers keep links with the countryside. Facilities in the country have lagged behind the town, but in Cuba special secondary boarding schools are being built in the country. The students are able to take advantage of the fresh air and open space.

▲ Aerial view of a housing scheme at Diego Martin, Trinidad. These houses are intended for middle-income families, but low-cost developments are becoming more common. The building industry is flourishing throughout the area.

◀ Life on the verandah in Port Antonio, Jamaica. The verandah is a traditional feature in many parts of the Caribbean and is ideal for the tropical climate. It provides shelter from both sun and rain, and may be built to catch any breezes which are blowing. The verandah can act as a dining room, living room, games room or a meeting place. It can even serve as a shop window for a dressmaker or small store. Living out on the verandah also has social advantages, adding a communal dimension to family life. Public buildings often have their verandahs too.

29

Commonwealth Caribbean

▶ Flags representing the 16 Commonwealth states and territories in the Caribbean area. Eight of them are British colonies or associated states. The other eight are independent sovereign states. In most of them the Queen of England, who is head of the Commonwealth, is also head of state. Only Trinidad and Tobago is a republic and has a president as head of state.

Anguilla

Bermuda

Bahamas

Trinidad and Tobago

Antigua

In place of empire

The Commonwealth now links the countries which used to be part of the British empire. Most of the member islands are in the eastern Caribbean, with only Jamaica and the Cayman Islands in the west. They share a common judicial system and a tradition of Westminster-style democracy. The Commonwealth islands also form a distinct and cohesive grouping in the region. They remain separate even from their English-speaking neighbour the United States, although recently Trinidad has been developing stronger links with the US.

British traditions

The education system is based on the British one. Students who want to go on to higher education take O-level and A-level exams, and until recently these have been set by British examination boards. In 1979 a new exam was launched by the Caribbean Examination Council with the aim of providing a syllabus suited to local needs. Although only five subjects were offered at O-level in the first year, 17,000 candidates entered from Trinidad alone. Higher education is provided at the University of the West Indies which is funded by a number of the Commonwealth Caribbean governments. Its main campuses are at Mona (Jamaica), St. Augustine (Trinidad) and Cave Hill (Barbados).

In 1970 the Commonwealth Caribbean governments joined together to launch the first regional population census. The participating countries all used identical census forms and made the count on the same day so that the statistics from each island could be readily compared.

Caricom

In 1973 the countries which had made up the Caribbean Free Trade Association (Carifta) transformed it into a new organization known as Caricom. Barbados now celebrates an annual holiday on the day the treaty was signed. The main aim of Caricom is to encourage trade within the region. The small islands have formed the Eastern Caribbean Common Market within Caricom, and many of them use a common currency – the Eastern Caribbean dollar. The WISCO shipping line and the LIAT airline are among the services sponsored by Caricom. The Caribbean Development Bank finances large-scale schemes.

Caricom is not intended to be a political unit. Before Jamaica became independent an attempt was made to unite ten Commonwealth Caribbean countries within a British West Indies Federation. It collapsed in 1961. Nevertheless the Caricom countries do co-ordinate their foreign policy wherever possible.

British Virgin Islands

St. Vincent

Barbados

Grenada

Montserrat

Cayman Islands

Dominica

Turks and Caicos Islands

St. Lucia

Jamaica

St. Kitts-Nevis

◄ Jamaica's governor-general delivering a speech to parliament, which sits in Gordon House, Kingston. The governor-general is Jamaican but represents the Queen of England. Here he is outlining the government's programme for a new session. Another piece of Westminster tradition is the ceremonial mace, which remains in place while parliament is sitting.

▲ T.A. Marryshow of Grenada was an early advocate of a single independent Caribbean-wide state made up of the English-speaking islands.

◄ H.M. Queen Elizabeth presenting degrees at the Trinidad campus of the University of the West Indies. The University was founded in 1948 and is now a strong influence holding the Commonwealth islands together.

► The Caribbean Community, usually known as Caricom, includes many of the Commonwealth islands as well as Belize and Guyana on the American mainland.

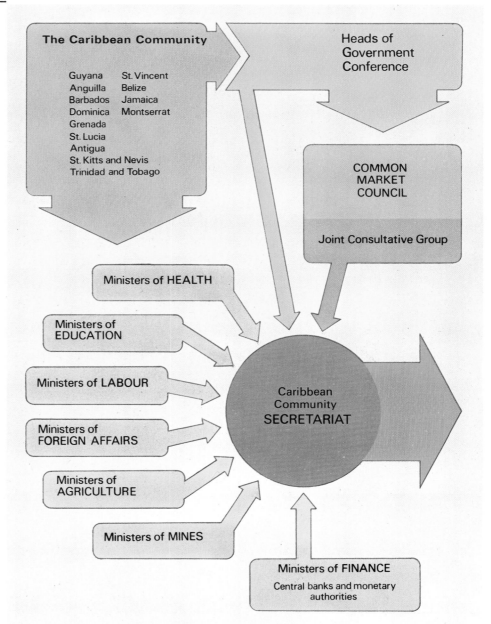

The Caribbean Community

Guyana St. Vincent
Anguilla Belize
Barbados Jamaica
Dominica Montserrat
Grenada
St. Lucia
Antigua
St. Kitts and Nevis
Trinidad and Tobago

Heads of Government Conference

COMMON MARKET COUNCIL

Joint Consultative Group

Ministers of HEALTH

Ministers of EDUCATION

Ministers of LABOUR

Ministers of FOREIGN AFFAIRS

Ministers of AGRICULTURE

Ministers of MINES

Caribbean Community SECRETARIAT

Ministers of FINANCE
Central banks and monetary authorities

Cuban vista

▼ In 1978 Cuba played host to the 11th Festival of Youth which brought together guests from all over the world. In the final parade shown here representatives from each country lined up against the background of a tableau formed by the coloured flags held up by the spectators. The figures depicted include a number of national heroes from Cuba's history. Havana is a well-established conference centre. United Nations seminars on housing and on apartheid have taken place there as did the 1979 meeting of the movement of non-aligned nations.

Revolution

Spanish rule over Cuba ended in 1898 when the United States defeated Spain. The island was occupied by US forces until 1902 when Cuba became independent. As a price for its withdrawal America insisted on keeping a military base in Cuba. The base is still there today.

The newly independent country was very strongly influenced by America and under Fulgencio Batista, who ruled Cuba from 1933 to 1944, its influence increased further. In 1953, a year after Batista regained power in a military coup, a group of rebels attacked the Moncada barracks. Fidel Castro, one of the rebel leaders, was arrested and exiled to Mexico. But the guerilla campaign against the government attracted strong support from workers and peasants. Castro returned from exile in 1956 as the guerilla advance continued.

Eventually the government was defeated, and on 1 January 1959 Castro, Camilo Cienfuegos and Che Guevara led a victorious parade through Havana. The new government nationalized nearly all agricultural land and private industry, much of which was owned by American interests. The United States, which had been Cuba's only major trading partner, imposed an economic blockade. This left the country isolated and starved of vital imports and Cuba turned to the Soviet Union for help.

Reconstruction

Before the revolution 600,000 Cubans were unemployed. The sugar industry, one of the main employers, offered only intermittent work. Today permanent employment is guaranteed in all branches of the economy.

By 1974 the infant mortality rate had been cut from 60 to 29 per thousand live births by raising health and sanitation standards and improving ante-natal care. Malaria, polio and diphtheria have all been eradicated. Members of the committees for the defence of the revolution administered one million doses of polio vaccine in 48 hours during the campaign. Life expectancy has risen from 55 to 70 years.

In a two-year programme in 1960–61 the illiteracy rate among adults was reduced from 23% to 2.9%. It is now even lower, making possible real progress in development. The social problems of the Caribbean have been extensively studied. In 1976 Cuba introduced a Family Code which aims to strengthen society by laying down the rights and responsibilities which apply within the family unit. The status of women has been raised by the educational work of the Federation of Cuban Women.

▶ The constitution of the Republic of Cuba was confirmed in a national referendum in 1975. Cubans qualify to vote when they reach 16 years of age. In a general election in 1976 10,000 delegates were elected to local and provincial assemblies. All delegates report to their constituents at regular public meetings. If a delegate's performance does not satisfy the constituents he or she can be made to resign. Each local assembly elects delegates to the National Assembly which is the highest authority in the land. The National Assembly elects a council of state which includes a president and 30 other members. The first president is Fidel Castro. New laws are debated by the National Assembly. They can be suggested by one of the autonomous organizations or by any group of people supported by the signatures of 10,000 voters.

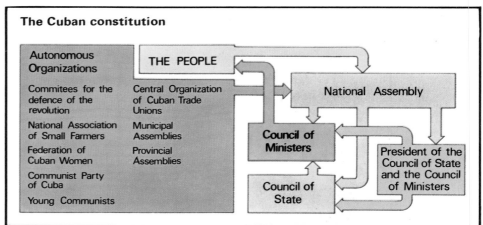

The Cuban constitution

Autonomous Organizations

THE PEOPLE

National Assembly

Commitees for the defence of the revolution

Central Organization of Cuban Trade Unions

National Association of Small Farmers

Municipal Assemblies

Federation of Cuban Women

Provincial Assemblies

Communist Party of Cuba

Young Communists

Council of Ministers

Council of State

President of the Council of State and the Council of Ministers

Mutual aid

Cuba has developed strong international links based on mutual aid. Cuban doctors and construction workers have aided Jamaica. Cuba has benefited in return from Jamaican techniques of coconut processing and expertise in hotel management. Cuba's newly revived tourist industry attracts mainly Canadian, Scandinavian and Soviet visitors.

As a developing country, Cuba offers aid in manpower rather than as money. For example, there are more Cuban doctors working in Africa than doctors from the World Health Organization. Special schools in Cuba educate students from Mozambique, Angola and elsewhere.

Cuba is a member of Comecon and trades on an equal basis with the industrialized communist countries. The Soviet Union buys Cuban sugar, and sells oil in return.

▶ This modern housing estate on the outskirts of Havana would not be out of place in any of the world's growing cities. Housing development in Cuba is proceeding fast, but still not fast enough to meet the country's needs. Every block of flats elects its own committee for the defence of the revolution. These committees participate in a wide range of community work.

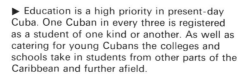

▲ A member of the rural health service stops his vehicle to talk to a colleague. All newly qualified doctors from Cuba's four medical schools work in the countryside for two years. Their services are augmented by students, workers and housewives who have received training in basic medical skills.

▶ Education is a high priority in present-day Cuba. One Cuban in every three is registered as a student of one kind or another. As well as catering for young Cubans the colleges and schools take in students from other parts of the Caribbean and further afield.

33

Cultural diversity

▼ A performance of *The King must Die* by the National Dance Theatre company of Jamaica under the direction of Rex Nettleford. Beryl McBurnie of Trinidad and Ivy Baxter of Jamaica are also pioneers of modern dance. Classical ballet is stronger in Cuba. The national company and their leading ballerina Alicia Alonso have made many successful tours overseas.

Fusion

The Caribbean is an area of cultural diversity and growth. This is celebrated in Carifesta, a festival of creative art which was first held in 1972. The 1979 festival attracted over 2,000 artists to Cuba. The rich variety arises from the cultural melting pot created when European and African nations met.

The written literature is characterized by strong links with the oral stories passed down by slaves. Many feature Anancy, a cunning spider who always outwits his enemies.

V. S. Naipaul made his name in the literary world with novels depicting British influence on his native Trinidad. Some of the best Caribbean writing has arisen out of political struggle. Claude McKay's widely acclaimed poem beginning, 'If we must die, let it not be like hogs,' was a cry on behalf of Black humanity. Aimé Césaire's concept of Black cultural consciousness has influenced writing all over the world.

Many artistic forms are combined. Nicolas Guillen, the National Poet of Cuba, was inspired by his country's folk music and some of his poems have been set to music. Roger Mais, the first novelist to acclaim the Rastafarian community, was also a dramatist and painter.

Play mas!

Theatre reaches its climax out on the streets. The carnival parades of the eastern Caribbean last for several days each year. Steel bands, with their attendant performers, compete for the approval of the crowds by portraying specially chosen themes. Equal

attention is given to dance, music and the special costumes.

Each island has its own style, with Trinidad staging the most elaborate performances. In Grenada the opening day features satirical characters lampooning establishment figures. In Martinique the end of the carnival is marked by the ceremonial burning of King Carnival.

The dance

All Caribbean music is danceable and dance forms abound. The Jonkonnu dancers, of the English-speaking Caribbean, wear distinctive costumes to play out their set roles. The Dominican Republic holds a special festival for the 'merengue', its most famous dance, while the Cuban rumba has penetrated every ballroom of the West. The 'belle aire', danced in Dominica, is distinguished by the drum beat following the dancer's movements instead of leading them.

▲ A scene from the world-famous Jamaican film *The Harder they Come*. It tells the story of a country boy who goes to Kingston looking for work and falls into bad company. The star is singer Jimmy Cliff and the film features several lively reggae numbers by Cliff and other artists.

◀ *Fantasy in Realism* by the Haitian painter and sculptor Jasmin Josef. This style of painting is characteristic of Haiti. It is ironic that Haiti, the poorest country in the Caribbean, should have some of the area's finest art treasures.

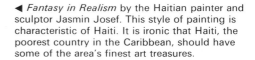

◀ The Trinidad carnival. Every year at carnival time normal life comes to a standstill as everyone's attention turns to the streets. The previous months are taken up with preparations. Costumes are made specially for each year's parade. These include matching sets for a whole group or spectacular set-pieces for one participant. The Roman Catholic origins of carnival are reflected in the islands where it is celebrated, all of which have a strong Catholic tradition. These include Grenada, St. Vincent, Dominica and Cuba.

▶ Louise Bennett-Coverley is a celebrated Jamaican story-teller, pantomime performer and folklorist. She has written numerous stories in Jamaican Creole. These have encouraged Jamaicans at home and abroad to take a pride in their own language. Much of her work concentrates on the impact of folk and popular language on literature. Other forms also have an important place in Caribbean literature. The Cuban-sponsored Casa de las Americas awards are presented every year to outstanding local authors.

Food from land and sea

A treat by any name

Like the people and the culture, Caribbean food is a mixture. Cassava, pineapple and coconuts were known to the early Arawaks and Caribs. Later arrivals which are now grown in quantity include yams, breadfruit, mangoes and citrus. Some types have been developed in the area, such as the grapefruit, the ugli and Jamaica's ortanique.

Many tropical fruits are now exported to temperate countries. Bananas, avocados, mangoes and limes from the Caribbean are familiar in Europe and North America. Some treats are not exportable. The refreshing coconut water from the immature green nut will quench any thirst. There is a unique satisfaction in chewing sugar juice out of freshly cut cane. The paw-paw is especially versatile. It is tasty whether cooked like a vegetable when still green or eaten ripe as a fruit. Preserves are made from local citrus fruits and guavas.

The variety of names can confuse visitors. Trinidadian bakes are popular through the Caribbean but in Jamaica they are known as Johnny cakes or fried dumplings. The christophene, a green pear-shaped vegetable, is known in Jamaica as cho-cho. Callalloo is a spinach-like vegetable, but in some places the same name is given to a nourishing soup containing okra and the dasheen 'sword' or young leaves. Pigeon or gungo peas are a rich source of protein. So are red peas, otherwise known as beans.

No meal is dull with so many local herbs and spices available. Nutmeg, annatto, pimento (allspice), mace, parsley and thyme all add their special flavours. The many varieties of burning hot chillies are an essential ingredient of several dishes, while ginger, lime juice and coconut also add their characteristic flavours.

Cocoa is a popular local drink. The beans are gently roasted and then ground in a mortar to form a chocolate butter. The mixture is seasoned with cinnamon and nutmeg, moulded into small cakes and left to dry in the sun. The hardened chocolate is grated into hot water or milk to make a delicious night-cap or a leisurely drink for Sunday 'brunch'.

The fish bill

Food production has suffered in the past from the heavy emphasis on export crops. None of the islands is self-sufficient in food. Fish imports are particularly costly for all.

Salt-fish is a major source of protein in the area. It can be stored indefinitely, and became popular as a 'convenience food' in the days before refrigeration. It is used in a variety of ways, but when combined with the Jamaican brand of ackee it makes a most tasty national delicacy.

▲ Market stall at Port Antonio in Jamaica carrying a range of local fruit. As well as its markets, Jamaica has numerous small shops which sell food and vegetables. Recently the government has stepped in to help with the distribution of fresh farm produce. It provides transport from collection depots to its own shops, which offer good service and a high standard of hygiene. Under this system the farmer is guaranteed a fair price and this encourages production. Studies undertaken by the Caribbean Food and Nutrition Institute have shown that locally grown food is as nutritious as it is varied.

▶ An open-air market in Haiti. The small-holders and farmers sell their produce here and are able to buy from other traders to meet their own needs. The large open-air markets which are held regularly all over Haiti are an important feature of the country's agricultural economy.

Caribbean cooking

▲ Rice and peas

Red kidney beans are the normal ingredient for this Jamaican dish. If pigeon peas are available they can be used instead.

Ingredients:
2 cups rice
1 cup red kidney beans
1 coconut
1 rasher of bacon, cut into pieces
salt, pepper, thyme

Grate the coconut to extract the juice or 'milk'.
Soak the beans overnight. Add the milk from the coconut to 3 cups of water and boil the beans in it for 2 hours. Add the bacon to the beans. Cook until tender. Add rice, salt, pepper and thyme and cook slowly until all the water is absorbed.

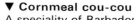

▼ Cornmeal cou-cou

A speciality of Barbados, where it is often served with flying fish. In other local variations the okras are replaced by coconut, green peppers or sweet corn.

Ingredients:
500 g okra
500 g cornmeal
2 tablespoons margarine
water, salt

Mix the cornmeal with 3 cups of salted water and stir well to make a smooth paste. Cut the stems off the okra and boil in 3 cups of salted water for 10 minutes. Drain the okra and add to the cornmeal paste. Continue to cook over a low heat, stirring continuously, until the mixture becomes stiff. Turn out into a dish and spread with margarine.

◄ Supermarkets are taking over from traditional shops especially in the cities. As in the United States, large supermarkets are being built everywhere. Those on the outskirts of town, where there is room for car parks, cater for customers with cars.

▲ A section of the famous floating market at Willemstad, Curaçao. Local fishermen sail right up to the roadside and sell their catch without leaving their boats. There is a fine selection of other produce too, especially fruit and vegetables.

Transport and communication

▲ Loading Geest bananas on to a banana boat in St. Lucia. The fast refrigerated vessels run by the banana companies are an essential link between the Caribbean plantations and their big markets in Europe and North America. In the days before mass air transport the banana boats also provided a reasonably cheap way of travelling to and from the Caribbean.

Road and rail
Internal travel is usually by road. On most islands the network is extensive with winding routes tackling the mountain areas. Puerto Rico has a comprehensive system of wide highways which were designed primarily to cope with the sugar traffic. Although roads are being improved throughout the area the overall standard is still poor.

Public transport is usually inadequate. The bus services use single-deckers which are rarely advertised in the tourist literature. In general there is a lack of investment in this vital domestic service. Exceptions to the rule are found in Bermuda, Cuba and the Puerto Rican capital San Juan which all have good bus services. In Freeport on Grand Bahama transport is provided by authentic red London double-deckers. In Trinidad there is a system of communal taxis to supplement the public transport.

Railways are only viable on the larger islands, though their terrain is often difficult to negotiate. Jamaica has two lines. One runs from Kingston to Montego Bay. The other branches off at Spanish Town and crosses the mountains to reach Albany and Port Antonio on the north coast. Haiti and the Dominican Republic have a few freight lines. The biggest system in the area is in Cuba, which boasted the first railway in Latin America. It has

a number of electrified lines and the network is still being modernized. Both Bermuda and Trinidad have abandoned rail travel and sold off the track. In Bermuda the route is used as a bridle path.

Airways
Good communications are needed to link the hundreds of Caribbean islands scattered over two million square kilometres of sea. Jamaica lies 1,800 kilometres from Barbados, yet they are both members of the same community. The six islands making up the Netherlands Antilles are particularly far-flung. Over 1,500 kilometres separate Saba, St. Eustatius and St. Maarten from the Aruba, Curaçao and Bonaire group off Venezuela.

In the past the air routes linked the main islands with Europe and America, and there were relatively few inter-island flights. This is changing and many islands now have their own airlines operating on a regional basis. Air Jamaica, Cubana (Cuba), BWIA (Trinidad) and International Caribbean Airways (Barbados) all operate internationally. So far the only joint venture is LIAT which is operated by the Caricom countries. Modern airports cater for the large aircraft which bring in foreign tourists. The tourist trade of St. Kitts has been transformed since an international airport was built at Golden Rock.

▶ Some of the schooners which make regular trips linking the Grenadines with St. Vincent in the north. Bequia, which is only 14 kilometres from St. Vincent, has a daily service. The people of St. Vincent have a strong sea-faring tradition and are skilled boat-builders.

Seaways

Some countries in the Caribbean are politically united but geographically separate. St. Vincent is the administrative centre for the northern Grenadines including Bequia, Canouan and Union. The schooner linking them with the capital at Kingstown is as essential as the Kingston–Montego Bay railway.

In general, shipping is now less important for passenger transport than for freight. The area is well served by international shipping lines and NAMUCAR, a shipping service owned by a number of Caribbean and Central American countries, recently came into operation. In 1975, when NAMUCAR was founded, 88% of the region's freight was carried in foreign-owned ships. NAMUCAR plans to acquire enough ships to have a total freight capacity of one million tons.

The islands are also connected by a sophisticated telecommunications network. The microwave system linking the eastern Caribbean islands from St. Thomas (US Virgin Islands) to Trinidad is among the most modern in the world. Radio and telephone systems are far in advance of other forms of local communications.

▲ The Caribbean has its share of traffic jams as can be seen from this view of Fort-de-France, Martinique. Heavy traffic is a feature of most of the towns and cities. In an effort to reduce traffic congestion and air pollution, restrictions are now being imposed on the size of cars.

▲ In Bermuda only one car per household is allowed. Strict limits are imposed on length and width and the maximum speed is 20 mph (32 km/h). Tourists cannot hire cars, but small motor cycles are available instead.

◄ Brightly painted buses are a particularly striking feature in Haiti. Buses provide the basic public transport throughout the Caribbean, though most of them are not so colourful.

A religious community

Believers all

The evidence of Christian influence is found everywhere in the Caribbean. Christian names are as common for places as for people. The old church parishes survive as units of local government in a number of islands including Barbados, Jamaica and Bermuda.

The largest denomination overall is Roman Catholic although Protestants dominate here and there as in the Bahamas and Jamaica. Many Christians worship in the Pentecostal tradition with an emphasis on joyful praise of God, obedience to the Bible and a strict lifestyle. The Catholic islands share a common tradition of carnival which originated as a last fling before the self-denial of Lent.

African values

Slaves were forbidden to practise their traditional religions but some of the runaway slaves or Maroons managed to preserve the old ways in their settlements. A religious cult of Kongolese origin called Kumina is still observed in the Cockpit Country of Jamaica.

The history of black suffering has recently led to new churches with a specifically black message. The Black Muslims are strong in Bermuda. Jamaica is the home of Rastafarianism, which is a Bible-based religion with stress on the Old Testament and the Book of Revelation. Rastafarians live by strict rules eating *ital* or organic food whenever possible. They take their name from Ras Tafari who was to become Emperor Haile Selassie of Ethiopia, and regard him as God Incarnate. The original Rastafarians opposed any organizational structure. But it is a rapidly growing religion and the various communities of believers differ according to religious, cultural or political emphasis.

Some folk religions combine old beliefs with Christianity. The Pocomania of Jamaica is one of these. In Haiti the influence of Voudou remains very strong.

Communion with life

The churches played a major role in providing education for all. The Nonconformists were specially keen that their converts should be able to read the Bible. Churches also played a pioneering role in medical services, and denominational hospitals are still common.

The Caribbean Council of Churches is an active force in the region. Its community development unit publishes the newspaper *Caribbean Contact* which is widely distributed and respected.

▲ A baptism ceremony in the Bahamas. Many Pentecostals as well as Baptists practise baptism by immersion. A number of Christian sects have a strong following in the Caribbean including the Seventh Day Adventists, Jehovah's Witnesses and the African Methodist Episcopal church.

▼ The Jama Masjid mosque near Port of Spain, Trinidad. The indentured workers who arrived from Asia in the nineteenth century introduced Islam to the Caribbean. The Hindu religion makes an impact too, especially during the feast of Diwali, which is celebrated out on the street in the same way as carnival.

▶ The Mikve Israel synagogue which was built in 1732 at Willemstad, Curaçao. Spanish and Portuguese Jews fled to the Caribbean at the time of the Spanish Inquisition in the early sixteenth century.

◄ A cemetery in Haiti. The many graveyards for people of different faiths are a reminder of the diverse backgrounds of the Caribbean people. Religious differences often coincide with social divisions, and this sometimes gives a religious aspect to disputes. In Jamaica during the battle for Emancipation some places of worship were destroyed in conflict between Anglicans and Nonconformists. In Haiti today the Voudou religion has a strong political element.

▼ Kapo is a self-taught painter and sculptor who has exhibited his work in London and New York. He is the 'shepherd' or leader of a Pocomania community in Jamaica and his work shows both religious and African influences. Some of his finest pieces are carved from lignum-vitae wood, obtained from the native guaiacum tree. These include the 70-centimetre high 'Angel', sometimes called the 'Winged Moon Man'.

Science and technology

International problems

In the Caribbean the inter-related activities of science and technology can mean survival itself. Nature does not respect national boundaries so international co-operation is required to study hurricanes and earthquakes.

The seismic research unit of the University of the West Indies monitors the earth's movements and attempts to predict earthquakes. Investigation of the underlying geology helps in other ways too. Quake-proof buildings can be designed if enough is known about the ground on which they are being built.

Scientific research

The biological sciences were the first to be applied in the Caribbean. From the days of colonial rule the health of the food crops was an important matter. The Imperial College of Tropical Agriculture in Trinidad and the Institute of Jamaica were set up for this purpose. Today similar research is carried out in the University of the West Indies and specialized institutes such as WINBAN.

Medical research is also actively pursued. Professor Carlos Finlay of Cuba was honoured posthumously by UNESCO for his work on the causes of yellow fever. The importance of traditional plant remedies is now recognized and in Jamaica several hundred species have been studied for their medicinal properties. Similar work is carried out at Cuba's Juan Tomas Rioz experimental station where animal products are also being tested as possible medicines.

The mysteries of the Bermuda Triangle have captured the world's attention. Several ships and aircraft have been mysteriously lost in the Triangle, which is the area of sea between Florida, Puerto Rico and Bermuda. A joint research project was mounted in the area by the United States and the Soviet Union. It found that no more ships or planes were lost than would normally be expected in such a busy area, and completely discounted suggestions that the losses were due to supernatural causes.

Energy and water

The increasing scarcity of oil is challenging technology all over the world including the Caribbean. One plentiful source of energy in the area is sunshine. In Jamaica solar heaters have been installed experimentally in hotels and public buildings. Cuba is beginning to generate electricity in nuclear power stations designed in the USSR and built with Soviet help.

Water is a scarce resource in many of the islands. Nassau's drinking water is brought by tanker from Andros Island 60 kilometres away. Fresh water can be obtained from the sea by desalinating it in flash distillation plants. These expensive installations are used in Antigua, Bermuda, the Netherlands Antilles and the Bahamas.

Marine research

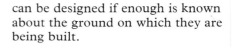

◀ Strong currents pass through the Caribbean Sea and the western Atlantic Ocean. They continue north-eastwards as the Gulf Stream which warms the coasts of north-west Europe. Marine science is a subject of growing interest in the Caribbean. The Cayman Trench to the south of the Cayman Islands is 7,680 metres deep, while the Milwaukee Deep north-east of the Dominican Republic is 9,200 metres deep. The St. George's research station on Bermuda was founded in 1903 and now attracts over 500 visiting scientists each year.

▼ Since 1977 Cuba has built the sophisticated Soviet-designed KTP-1 sugar-cane harvester at a new plant set up with Soviet assistance at Holguin. In return most of Cuba's sugar production goes to the USSR and other Comecon countries.

▼ A class of Cuban school students wiring up printed-circuit boards. The periods of work which are undertaken in all Cuban schools are used to provide basic technological skills. Instructors are on hand to supervise the work. In this way the students are given access to complex and expensive equipment which the schools would not otherwise be able to afford.

▶ An assistant performing routine analysis at the Windward Islands Banana Association (WINBAN) laboratories. Research centres like these are vital to countries which depend on agricultural exports. An epidemic plant disease can blight an entire island and set its economy back for years. Special strains have been developed to suit local conditions.

▲ In touch with the world through the Antigua switchboard of Britain's Cable and Wireless company. The agreement which supplied sophisticated British communications technology to the islands of the eastern Caribbean is considered a model of its kind.

◀ Veterinary science has an important part to play. The Jamaican Hope cattle seen here are a dairy breed which yield large quantities of milk. The breed was developed in Jamaica by Dr T. P. Lecky who was awarded the country's Order of Merit for his work. He also developed the Jamaica Black, which is a beef-producing breed. The Caribbean climate presents problems for cattle farmers as most other breeds do not thrive in it. A tropical strain of the Holstein dairy cattle has been bred in Cuba.

Industries large and small

Light manufacture

In the sixteenth-century city of Trinidad on the south coast of Cuba traditional hand-woven straw hats are still made today. Straw work is a cottage industry common to the whole region. Sisal is used in Cozumel while Dominica is famous for its king-size mats. Jamaican homes often display evidence of skill with Jippi Jappa straw.

Many of the islands have light-manufacturing enterprises or factories where imported items are assembled for re-export. These often rely on low wage levels to compensate for increased transport costs. Both types are relatively cheap to set up and have been encouraged by many countries as a way of modernizing themselves. These attempts have not always succeeded as many of the factories have only operated for a short while before closing.

Minerals

Mineral extraction has been important in the larger islands for some time. Bauxite is a key industry in Jamaica and is also mined in Haiti and the Dominican Republic. Cuba has deposits of copper, nickel, manganese and chrome, and one of the largest reserves of iron ore in the world. Rock salt and gypsum are both mined in the southern part of the Dominican Republic.

Trinidad is a producer of crude oil. This ready source of foreign exchange has helped Trinidad build up its industries, and it is now the most industrialized of the eastern Caribbean islands.

Jamaica seeks co-operation with her neighbours in the processing of her bauxite ore into aluminium. The raw material can be exported but its value increases with each step it takes towards finished goods. Aluminium smelting requires a great deal of energy, and Jamaica lacks fuel resources. An aluminium smelter has therefore been built in Venezuela. It uses local oil to refine Jamaican bauxite. A novel trade agreement between the two countries gives Jamaica part ownership of the plant. Trinidad also plans a smelter fuelled by her own oil.

Heavy investment

Heavy industries help a country to be independent but they are expensive to set up. The oil refining industry is stimulated by demand from the United States. Old-established refineries in Aruba, Curaçao and Trinidad have been joined by a new complex in the Bahamas. Locally produced oil is supplemented by crude oil from Venezuela and the Middle East.

Trinidad has an important petro-chemical complex. Its products are nearly all exported to the United States.

Cuba's modern fishing fleet ventures as far as the well-stocked North Atlantic fishing grounds. Cuba is also building up a modern merchant fleet which includes vessels of over 20,000 tons. Until recently these were maintained and repaired in European and Asian shipyards which involved a return trip of several weeks. Now the work is done in the Curaçao yards which have a new dry dock for ships of up to 120,000 tons.

◄ The salt pans on Anguilla are separated from the sea by a narrow spit of sand. Salt is obtained from sea water by evaporation in the bright sun and is one of the few natural resources of this tiny island. Salt was one of the region's major attractions to the early European explorers. The Dutch took St. Maarten and Bonaire in order to obtain salt to use for preserving fish caught at home. There are still substantial salt deposits in the Turks and Caicos islands and on Great Inagua in the Bahamas.

▼ The Pitch Lake in southern Trinidad is just that — a lake made entirely of pitch. It is over 20 hectares in area and 60 metres deep, although the level has dropped as pitch has been removed. The lake is one of the world's few reserves of natural pitch. Over 15 million tons of it have been taken from the lake since it was first exploited at the beginning of the twentieth century. The pitch is widely used locally for surfacing roads and is exported for the same purposes. Pitch is a liquid but it is so viscous that lorries can be driven out on to the hot black surface of the lake.

◄ The Kirkvine works near Mandeville, Jamaica, where bauxite is converted to alumina in the first stage of the production of aluminium. Jamaica is the world's second largest producer of bauxite and alumina and supplies about half of the United States' requirements. It is of enormous importance to Jamaica's economy. In 1977 alumina and bauxite together represented 70% of Jamaica's exports.

▼ The oil refinery at Willemstad, Curaçao is operated by the Shell company which is based in Europe. It was opened in 1918 and was established specifically to refine oil produced in Venezuela. In 1929 it was joined by the American-owned refinery in Aruba. The refineries have been a major source of employment in Aruba, Curaçao and Bonaire and have attracted workers from Grenada and St. Kitts as well as the more remote Dutch islands of Saba, St. Maarten and St. Eustatius.

Achievement in sport

Olympic stars

The Caribbean has a fine record of Olympic achievement, especially on the track and in the boxing ring. The Jamaican team of Wint, McKenley, Laing and Rhoden set the pace even before independence, when they stormed to a world record in the 4 × 100 yards relay at the Helsinki games in 1952. Competition is keen throughout the region, and reaches a climax in the Central American and Caribbean Games held every four years.

Cuba is the leading sporting nation of the area thanks to her comprehensive sports programme. It involves early selection and specialized training, and draws on help from a highly developed sports medicine unit. A network of basic sports schools is being developed to train children who show exceptional talent.

Students at the sports schools pursue their normal studies but receive special sports training instead of the regular periods of manual work undertaken by students at other schools. The whole Caribbean can be proud of Cuba's showing in the Pan-American Games held in Puerto Rico in 1979. She finished second, ahead of all the continental countries except the United States.

By contrast, the training facilities in most of the other countries are poor. Many athletes are forced to leave in order to take advantage of the nearby North American circuit. Some European teams are strengthened by athletes of Caribbean origin whose parents have settled abroad.

Cricket ritual

Cricket is the game most strongly associated with the English-speaking Caribbean. It was introduced from England in 1850 and rapidly caught on at all levels of society. Even so, it was not until the 1960s that fully integrated teams based on merit were chosen for international competition. The game commands great interest throughout the area. During the annual Cup Match in Bermuda there is a two-day public holiday so that everyone can watch.

At all matches the spectators are well-informed and passions can run very high. This is especially true at test matches between England and the West Indies. The crowd gets enormous satisfaction out of seeing the old colonial power beaten at its own game by the local team. In 1979 the West Indies team beat England in the final of the World Cup knockout competition which took place at Lord's cricket ground in London.

Outside the Commonwealth islands other spectator sports are popular. Football is Haiti's national game, while the Cubans prefer American-style baseball. Horse racing is popular in Jamaica and Puerto Rico with betting as a side attraction. Cycling, an old-established sport, now takes place on the road in Caribbean-wide meets.

Keeping fit

In Puerto Rico archaeologists have uncovered the site of a playing field which shows that ball games have been played in the Caribbean since the days of the Arawaks. Today netball, baseball, basketball, softball, volleyball and football continue the tradition. Schools provide a wide choice of sports and for the adults there are usually a number of local teams.

Cuba recognizes the value of exercise for health, and everyone is encouraged to participate in local keep-fit classes. Bermuda claims the honour of having introduced the game of tennis to the United States. Football is very popular, and inter-island tournaments

▼ An informal game of cricket under way in Barbados. Cricket is not just a sport to watch but a game to be played. Barbados is the focal point of West Indies cricket and has produced a number of outstanding players in recent years. These include fast bowlers Hall and Griffith and all-rounder Gary Sobers.

are organized regularly. Teams from Guadeloupe and Martinique meet every year for the traditional Easter Sunday soccer match.

Boxing attracts wide attention, notably in Puerto Rico which has produced world-class champions. Polo and golf are popular with a wealthy minority. The sea is an ideal place for recreation. Swimming, water-skiing and scuba diving are all popular pursuits.

▲ Playing netball at the Jamaican school named after the athlete Don Quarrie. Strong school support for the game is reflected in the high standard of women's netball teams. The Trinidad and Tobago national team frequently appears in international events.

▼ Football is a popular game throughout the Caribbean. Though it cannot compete with cricket as a crowd-puller there are a number of local competitions between amateur teams.

▲ Hasely Crawford of Trinidad and Tobago, who won the Olympic Gold Medal for the 100 metres at the 1976 Montreal Games. The Caribbean excelled in athletics at Montreal. Don Quarrie of Jamaica won the 200 metres and Alberto Juantorena of Cuba was a double winner of the 400- and 800-metre events.

Life set to music

Voices

Music is central to Caribbean life. People do not just sit and listen to it – they make it. New words, new tunes, even new instruments are created. All reflect life as it is lived, making it real music of the people.

The church choir provides the first stage for many performers. All denominations have a strong singing tradition. The slaves of West African origin were used to worshipping God through song and continued to do so after they had accepted Christianity. In the past they sang to protest at their captivity. The Haitian drums sounded throughout Saint-Domingue in 1791 calling the slaves to revolt. The drums are still heard today at the 1 January anniversary celebrations of that revolution.

Creativity reaches a high point in Trinidadian calypso. It is a blend of Asian, Spanish and Venuzuelan elements with strong influence from the troubadour or *kaiso* tradition of West Africa. Political movements and parties do not ignore music either. 'La Borinquena' is a rousing independence anthem taking its title from the original name for Puerto Rico. It still arouses powerful emotions after over 100 years.

The sound of steel

The drum provides the dominant musical sound, although guitars have a long history in the Spanish-speaking islands. A totally new instrument was created in Trinidad in the 1940s – the steel drum. It happened during the Second World War when carnival was banned. Some local musicians, looking around for a source of music, made the first steel drums or 'pans' out of scrap oil drums. The metal is beaten out in such a way that a variety of notes can be played by striking different parts of the drum. Steel bands are now an established feature of carnival. The instrument is quite versatile and both classical and calypso numbers can be played to the tune of steel.

▼ The Mighty Sparrow is a Grenada-born calypso singer and the most famous exponent of this popular musical style. Calypso originates in Trinidad but its wry comments on life cover the entire English-speaking Caribbean. Good singers are composers too, and the best can make up a new song on the spot. Most of them deal with current events or variations on the man-woman theme. Calypsos are produced specially for carnival when the most popular are heard all over Trinidad. Sometimes two singers compete on stage to see whose instant verses will please the audience best. Calypso has counterparts in the Spanish-speaking Caribbean, notably the *salsa* of Cuba and Puerto Rico.

▶ A Trinidad steel band flying the flag of BWIA, the country's national airline. Pan music is an original twentieth-century contribution to musical art and one of the boldest contemporary developments in the world of percussion. It is a tribute to the inventiveness of the people of Trinidad from whose oil industry this musical revolution emerged. The drums are tuned by beating out the metal. This highly skilled task can take several days for each drum.

Reggae is one of Jamaica's best-known exports with superstar Bob Marley as popular abroad as at home. Its thumping guitar beat originally came from the Bura drums adopted by the Rastafarians. The words of current reggae favourites tell everybody listening about the struggles of every-day life. The Rasta religious message remains the strongest influence, though on the international scene reggae lyrics are less dependent on it.

'Toasting' is another musical style from Jamaica. Disc jockeys in the clubs improvise on top of imported American blues records to suit Jamaican pace and taste. The DJs are known as 'toasters'. In areas where few people can afford individual record players the sound man is on hand with his amplified sound system.

Side by side with new songs and rhythms, the old folk tunes are still sung and enjoyed. Harry Belafonte popularized Jamaican songs in the 1950s, though his recordings are very different from the Creole originals.

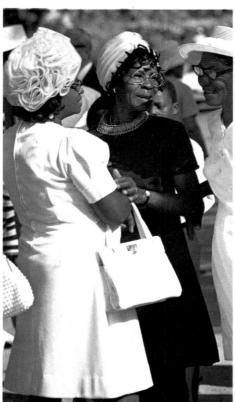

▲ Versatile artist Brother Everard of the Rastafarian faith works from his home on the outskirts of Jamaica's capital Kingston. He makes musical instruments when he is not painting intricate motifs and landscapes, two of his favourite themes. The Rastaman is more commonly associated with reggae, a form of music which is enjoyed by all sections of Jamaica's varied community.

◄ Going to church is a weekly ritual, and wearing Sunday best is a part of it. Secular music has been deeply influenced by the church. Conservative European forms merge with the spontaneous music of the Pentecostal church with choruses accompanied by hand-clapping and the tambourine. Among major exponents of this branch of Caribbean music are the Barbados Police Band and Jamaica's Frats Quintet. The sounds of the well-known Toots and the Maytals are rooted in the Pocomania religious tradition.

The Caribbean and the world

Messages and messengers

The Caribbean has never lacked eloquent representation on the world stage. Its heroes were acclaimed at Carifesta '76 in Jamaica: Toussaint L'Ouverture, leader of Haiti's rebel army; Simon Bolivar, the liberator of Spanish America; Benito Juarez, the Mexican patriot; José Marti, apostle of the Cuban revolution; and Marcus Garvey, the world-wide anti-racist campaigner. Together they symbolize the traditional militancy of Caribbean culture and the power of its message.

Frantz Fanon of Martinique became a spokesman for all colonial peoples through his book *Wretched of the Earth*. His opinions grew out of experience in his home country, medical training in France and work as a psychiatrist in Algeria during the guerilla war against French rule in the 1950s.

Internationalism

The Caribbean spirit of internationalism was shown in its support for the Allies in the Second World War against the fascist regimes of Germany, Italy and Japan. In 1962 a confrontation took place between the United States and the Soviet Union following the installation of Soviet nuclear missiles in Cuba. This brought the world to the brink of nuclear war but today the talk is of peace. Caribbean governments have spoken out strongly at the United Nations in favour of disarmament. A nuclear-free zone covers Latin America and the Caribbean.

The majority of independent Caribbean countries are members of the Organization of American States and enjoy traditional ties of friendship with the United States. Cuba's ties are with the Soviet Union and competition between the two super-powers continues to generate tension in the area. Nevertheless local co-operation and friendship across the East–West divide are growing. The small Caribbean states gain security and confidence by establishing links with friendly countries in the rest of the world.

▼ The headquarters of the Organization of African Unity at Addis Ababa, capital of Ethiopia. Much of the inspiration for the OAU came from Caribbean figures such as George Padmore, C. L. R. James and Aimé Césaire.

◄ Bob Marley, the turbulent Rastafarian reggae artist. Marley's music has brought him fame around the world and done much to spread the Rastafarian message from Jamaica into the rest of the world. The Rastafarian creed has peace and love as its central elements together with the deity of the late Emperor Haile Selassie of Ethiopia. It recognises Africa as the true home of all Black people and thus shows clear links with the teachings of Marcus Garvey. Rastas liken the world they know to Biblical Babylon. Many see Marley as the Messenger. His status as superstar gives him the opportunity to uphold the word of Jah, the Biblical command not to cut off one's hair and to expose the evils of Babylon.

▲ Amy Jacques, the second wife of Marcus Garvey, continued to spread Garvey's ideas until her own death in 1973. It is a result of her work that Garvey is now a hero in his native Jamaica and his memory is respected through-out the world. In 1909, when he was 22, Marcus Garvey left Jamaica. He had already become aware of the unjust treatment of Black people in Jamaica and found that Blacks received the same treatment everywhere. In the United States he founded the Universal Negro Improvement Association which aimed to unite Black people throughout the world. By 1921 the UNIA had millions of supporters, and people came from all over the world to a rally in New York. The previous year Garvey founded the Black Star shipping line which was intended to strengthen links with Africa. He also set up factories and businesses which were designed to enable American Blacks to become economically independent. But Garvey lacked business acumen, and these enterprises eventually failed. Garvey served a five-year prison sentence following breaches of postal laws. In 1929 he returned to Jamaica and a hostile reception from the press. He organized the Peoples Political Party but was defeated in elections the following year. He finally left Jamaica in 1935 to spend his last years in England, where he died in 1940. Garvey never set foot on the African continent for which he lived, but his ideas have inspired African leaders such as Kwame Nkrumah, Ghana's first president, as well as American poets and revolutionaries. In 1964 his body was brought home to Jamaica for re-burial, and he is now recognized as a national hero.

Reference: *Human and physical geography*

▶ States and territories of the Caribbean. The maps are not to scale. Each one shows the name (in *italics*) of the main island and of the more important lesser islands in the group. The capital of the island or group is also marked. In each caption the name of the state is followed by its political status, with the date of independence where applicable. The area given is the combined area of all the islands of the group. Population figures are taken from the latest official census, or from more recent estimates where these are available. Where there is more than one language, the official language is given first.

The Caribbean islands lie mainly within the northern tropical zone. The Tropic of Cancer passes between Cuba and Florida, and cuts through the Bahamas. Temperatures are fairly steady throughout the year. Total rainfall varies considerably from place to place within each island. The mountainous islands of the eastern Caribbean receive most of their rainfall on the windward (eastern) side.

Bermuda is geographically separate from the other islands. There is a marked difference between summer and winter temperatures, although the influence of the Gulf Stream keeps its winters mild.

The total area of the Caribbean islands is about 230,000 square kilometres. The total population is about 25,000,000. Population density varies greatly from island to island. The Bahamas have less than ten people for each square kilometre of land, while Bermuda has over 1,000.

▼ Total rainfall varies but the seasonal pattern is the same everywhere with a wet season in the second half of the year. There are noticeable differences between summer and winter in the north and west, while in the south temperatures are steady throughout the year.

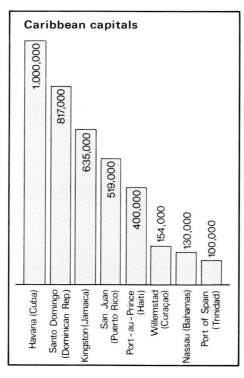

Caribbean capitals

- 1,000,000 — Havana (Cuba)
- 817,000 — Santo Domingo (Dominican Rep.)
- 635,000 — Kingston (Jamaica)
- 519,000 — San Juan (Puerto Rico)
- 400,000 — Port-au-Prince (Haiti)
- 154,000 — Willemstad (Curaçao)
- 130,000 — Nassau (Bahamas)
- 100,000 — Port of Spain (Trinidad)

▲ Eight capital cities have populations of 100,000 or more. Ponce and Bayamon in Puerto Rico and the Cuban cities of Marianao, Santiago de Cuba, San Miguel de Padron, Camagüey, Santa Clara and Guantanamo also have six-figure populations.

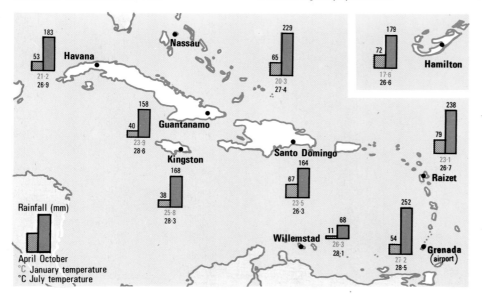

Rainfall (mm)
April October
°C January temperature
°C July temperature

Anguilla
British associated state
Area: 90 sq.km.
Population: 6,500
Language: English

Antigua
British associated state
Area: 440 sq.km.
Population: 65,500
Languages: English, Creole

Aruba
Part of Netherlands Antilles
Area: 190 sq.km.
Population: 61,700
Languages: Dutch, Papiamento

Bahamas
Independent (1973)
Area: 11,400 sq.km.
Population: 175,000
Language: English

Barbados
Independent (1966)
Area: 430 sq.km.
Population: 238,000
Language: English

Bermuda
British crown colony
Area: 53 sq.km.
Population: 58,500
Language: English

Bonaire
Part of Netherlands Antilles
Area: 288 sq.km.
Population: 8,200
Languages: Dutch, Papiamento

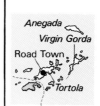

British Virgin Islands
British dependent territory
Area: 170 sq.km.
Population: 9,800
Language: English

Cayman Islands
British dependent territory
Area: 260 sq.km.
Population: 10,500
Language: English

Haiti
Independent (1804)
Area: 27,700 sq.km.
Population: 4,330,000
Languages: French,
Creole

St. Kitts-Nevis
British associated state
Area: 310 sq.km.
Population: 57,000
Languages: English,
Creole

Cuba
Independent (1902)
Area: 110,900 sq.km.
Population: 8,569,000
Language: Spanish

Jamaica
Independent (1962)
Area: 11,400 sq.km.
Population: 1,849,000
Languages: English,
Creole

St. Lucia
Independent (1979)
Area: 603 sq.km.
Population: 100,900
Languages: English,
Creole

Martinique
French territory
Area: 1,100 sq.km.
Population: 325,000
Languages: French,
Creole

St. Maarten
Part of Netherlands
Antilles
Area: 34 sq.km.
Population: 9,800
Languages: Dutch,
English

Curaçao
Part of Netherlands
Antilles
Area: 440 sq.km.
Population: 152,200
Languages: Dutch,
Papiamento

Mexico — **Cozumel**
Part of Mexico
Area: 400 sq.km.
Population: 20,000
Language: Spanish

**St. Vincent and the
Grenadines**
Independent (1979)
Area: 430 sq.km.
Population: 87,300
Language: English

Dominica
Independent (1978)
Area: 790 sq.km.
Population: 70,500
Languages: English,
Creole

Montserrat
British crown colony
Area: 84 sq.km.
Population: 11,700
Language: English

Trinidad & Tobago
Independent (1962)
Area: 5,130 sq.km.
Population: 941,000
Languages: English,
Creole

Dominican Republic
Independent (1844)
Area: 48,700 sq.km
Population: 4,006,000
Languages: Spanish,
various Creoles

Puerto Rico
Associated with United
States
Area: 8,900 sq.km.
Population: 2,712,000
Language: Spanish

Turks & Caicos Islands
British dependent territory
Area: 430 sq.km.
Population: 5,700
Language: English

Grenada
Independent (1974)
Area: 345 sq.km
Population: 93,800
Languages: English,
Creole

Saba
Part of Netherlands
Antilles
Area: 13 sq.km.
Population: 970
Languages: Dutch,
English

**United States Virgin
Islands**
US territory
Area: 350 sq.km.
Population: 62,500
Language: English

Guadeloupe (including
Désirade, Les Saintes,
St. Martin,
St. Barthélémy)
French territory
Area: 1,700 sq.km
Population: 324,000
Languages: French,
Creole

St. Eustatius
Part of Netherlands
Antilles
Area: 21 sq.km.
Population: 1,450
Languages: Dutch,
English

Venezuela — **Margarita**
Part of Venezuela
Area: 1,040 sq.km.
Population: 119,000
Language: Spanish

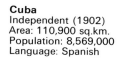

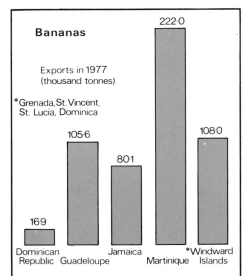

Bananas

Exports in 1977
(thousand tonnes)

*Grenada, St. Vincent, St. Lucia, Dominica

16·9	105·6	80·1	222·0	108·0
Dominican Republic	Guadeloupe	Jamaica	Martinique	*Windward Islands

The Caribbean supplied only a small fraction of the world total of 6.8 million tonnes for 1977. Production is concentrated on small islands for whom the crop is of considerable importance.

Source: FAO

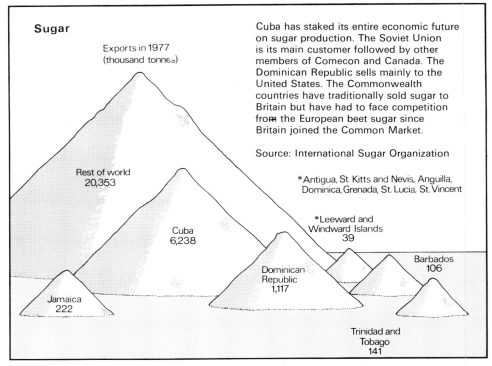

Sugar

Exports in 1977
(thousand tonnes)

Rest of world 20,353
Cuba 6,238
Dominican Republic 1,117
Jamaica 222
*Leeward and Windward Islands 39
Barbados 106
Trinidad and Tobago 141

Cuba has staked its entire economic future on sugar production. The Soviet Union is its main customer followed by other members of Comecon and Canada. The Dominican Republic sells mainly to the United States. The Commonwealth countries have traditionally sold sugar to Britain but have had to face competition from the European beet sugar since Britain joined the Common Market.

Source: International Sugar Organization

*Antigua, St. Kitts and Nevis, Anguilla, Dominica, Grenada, St. Lucia, St. Vincent

Sugar-cane cultivation remains a key factor for the economic development of many of the islands. Large-scale plantations still account for the majority of production, though in some islands small farmers grow cane to sell to the mills. The flatter lowland areas are more suitable for the establishment of large plantations while small farms predominate in the steeper upland areas. On the British and French islands sugar was cultivated on large slave-based plantations from the earliest days.

In the Spanish colonies most of the land was divided into small peasant farms. Large plantations did not begin to appear there until the nineteenth century. Market-gardening is a major occupation, especially in the smaller islands. Some islands still rely on imported supplies of fresh water and have no surplus which can be used for irrigation.

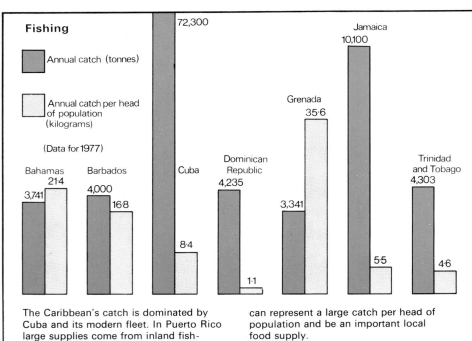

Fishing

- Annual catch (tonnes)
- Annual catch per head of population (kilograms)

(Data for 1977)

	Bahamas	Barbados	Cuba	Dominican Republic	Grenada	Jamaica	Trinidad and Tobago
Annual catch (tonnes)	3,741	4,000	72,300	4,235	3,341	10,100	4,303
Catch per head (kg)	214	16·8	8·4	1·1	35·6	5·5	4·6

The Caribbean's catch is dominated by Cuba and its modern fleet. In Puerto Rico large supplies come from inland fish-farms. The smaller islands' small landings can represent a large catch per head of population and be an important local food supply.
Source: FAO

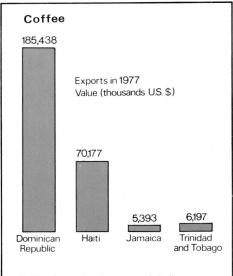

Coffee

Exports in 1977
Value (thousands U.S. $)

Dominican Republic	Haiti	Jamaica	Trinidad and Tobago
185,438	70,177	5,393	6,197

Coffee flourishes in equatorial climates but only at high altitude. It is therefore the larger and more mountainous islands which are the area's only coffee exporters.

Source: International Coffee Organization

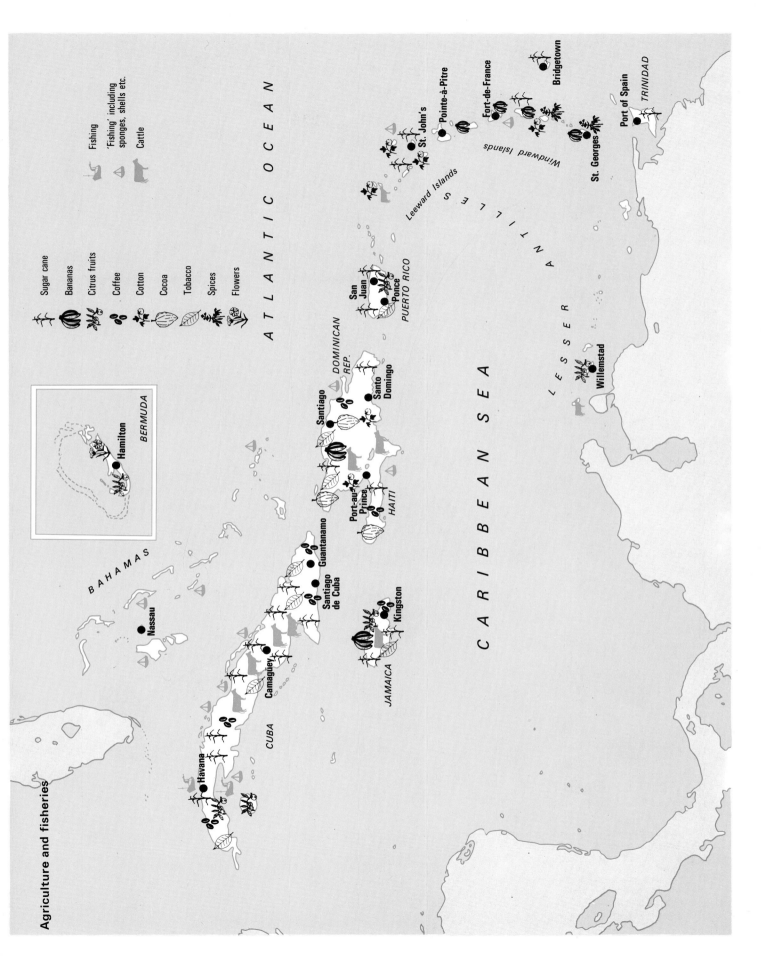

Agriculture and fisheries

Sugar cane
Bananas
Citrus fruits
Coffee
Cotton
Cocoa
Tobacco
Spices
Flowers

Fishing
'Fishing' including sponges, shells etc.
Cattle

ATLANTIC OCEAN

BERMUDA
Hamilton

BAHAMAS
Nassau

CUBA
Havana
Camagüey
Santiago de Cuba
Guantánamo

JAMAICA
Kingston

HAITI
Port-au-Prince

DOMINICAN REP.
Santiago
Santo Domingo

PUERTO RICO
San Juan
Ponce

Leeward Islands
St. John's
Pointe-à-Pitre
Fort-de-France

Windward Islands
Bridgetown
St. Georges
Port of Spain
TRINIDAD

LESSER ANTILLES

Willemstad

CARIBBEAN SEA

55

Reference: *Wealth, welfare and employment*

Currency

Puerto Rico, the US Virgin Islands, the British Virgin Islands and the Turks and Caicos Islands all use the US dollar as their unit of currency. Some other states link the value of their own currency to the US dollar:

Bahamas (1 Bahama dollar = 1 US $)

Barbados (1 Barbados dollar = 2 US $)

Bermuda (1 Bermuda dollar = 1 US $)

Cayman Islands (1 C.I. dollar = 1.2 US $)

Dominican Republic (1 peso = 1 US $)

Haiti (1 gourde = 0.2 US $)

Anguilla, Antigua, Dominica, Grenada, Montserrat, St. Lucia, St. Vincent and St. Kitts-Nevis all use the Eastern Caribbean dollar which is valued at 0.37 US $. Aruba, Curaçao, Bonaire, Saba, St. Eustatius, and St. Maarten all use the Netherlands Antilles guilder (1 N.A.F1 = 0.556 US $). Guadeloupe and Martinique use the French franc. Each of the three remaining islands has its own currency:

Cuba (1 peso = 1.35 US $)

Jamaica (1 Jamaican dollar = 0.58 US $)

Trinidad and Tobago (1 T.T. dollar = 0.417 US $)

(All values are for 1 January 1979.)

International groupings

There are a number of local and regional organizations to which Caribbean nations belong:

Latin American Economic System (SELA) Founded in 1975. Total of 25 members.

Caribbean Development and Co-operation Committee (CDC) Aims for co-ordination and consultation in tourism, public health, transfer of technology and related areas.

Latin American Energy Organization (OLADE) Includes Haiti, Jamaica, Cuba and Trinidad.

Caribbean Multinational Shipping Enterprise (NAMUCAR) Founder members include Jamaica and Cuba.

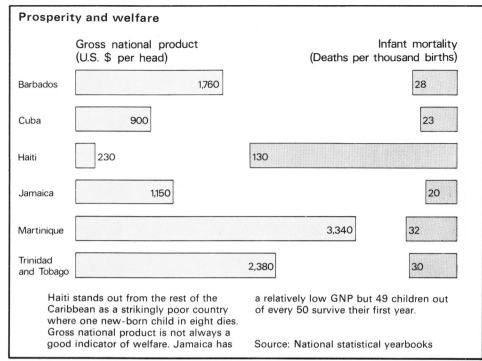

Prosperity and welfare

Haiti stands out from the rest of the Caribbean as a strikingly poor country where one new-born child in eight dies. Gross national product is not always a good indicator of welfare. Jamaica has a relatively low GNP but 49 children out of every 50 survive their first year.

Source: National statistical yearbooks

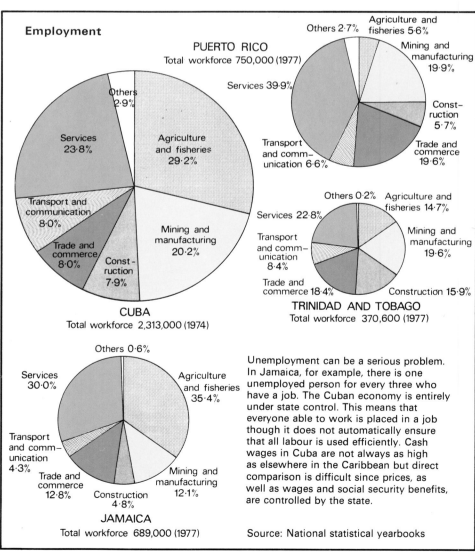

Employment

Unemployment can be a serious problem. In Jamaica, for example, there is one unemployed person for every three who have a job. The Cuban economy is entirely under state control. This means that everyone able to work is placed in a job though it does not automatically ensure that all labour is used efficiently. Cash wages in Cuba are not always as high as elsewhere in the Caribbean but direct comparison is difficult since prices, as well as wages and social security benefits, are controlled by the state.

Source: National statistical yearbooks

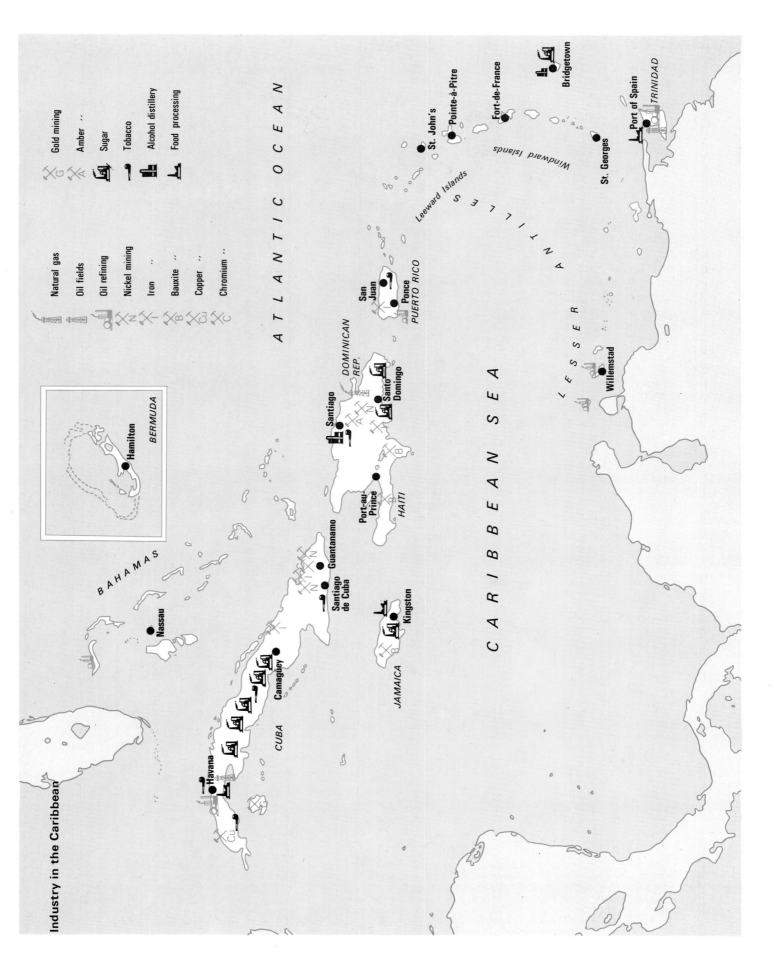

Industry in the Caribbean

Gold mining G
Amber A
Sugar
Tobacco
Alcohol distillery
Food processing

Natural gas
Oil fields
Oil refining
Nickel mining N
Iron N
Bauxite B
Copper Cu
Chromium C

BERMUDA
Hamilton

BAHAMAS
Nassau

CUBA
Havana
Camagüey
Santiago de Cuba
Guantanamo

JAMAICA
Kingston

HAITI
Port-au-Prince

DOMINICAN REP.
Santiago
Santo Domingo

PUERTO RICO
San Juan
Ponce

ATLANTIC OCEAN

CARIBBEAN SEA

St. John's
Pointe-à-Pitre
Fort-de-France
Bridgetown
St. Georges
Port of Spain
TRINIDAD

Willemstad

Leeward Islands
Windward Islands
LESSER ANTILLES

57

Reference: *Trade and tourism*

The Caribbean's main trading relations are with Western Europe and North America. Regional trade accounts for only a small percentage although efforts are being made to increase it. In 1977 one-quarter of Barbados's exports were within Caricom. Free-trade areas and duty-free shops are a feature of many islands. The whole of Margarita island is a free-trade zone.

Most Latin American and Caribbean countries are primary producers of mineral ores or agricultural goods. They share the problems of under-development. For manufactured items they rely mainly on imports and are at an increasing disadvantage in the world economic system. In 1965 Jamaica could buy one imported tractor for the price of 21 tons of sugar sold abroad. In 1979 it was necessary to sell 59 tons of sugar to pay for one tractor. Many Caribbean countries support the movement for a New International Economic Order. This political movement aims to reduce the dominating role of the industrialized nations over the primary producers and thereby increase the prosperity of the under-developed nations.

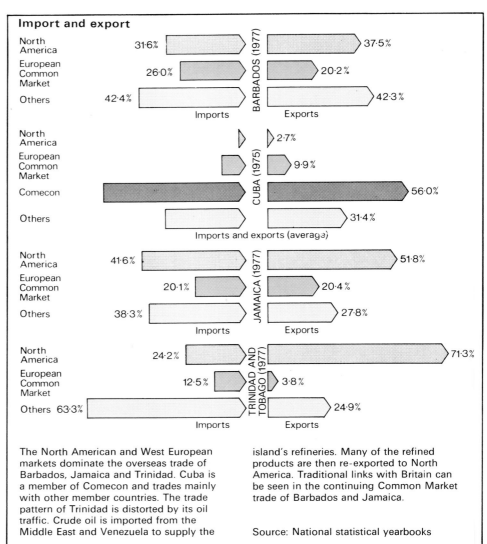

Import and export

The North American and West European markets dominate the overseas trade of Barbados, Jamaica and Trinidad. Cuba is a member of Comecon and trades mainly with other member countries. The trade pattern of Trinidad is distorted by its oil traffic. Crude oil is imported from the Middle East and Venezuela to supply the island's refineries. Many of the refined products are then re-exported to North America. Traditional links with Britain can be seen in the continuing Common Market trade of Barbados and Jamaica.

Source: National statistical yearbooks

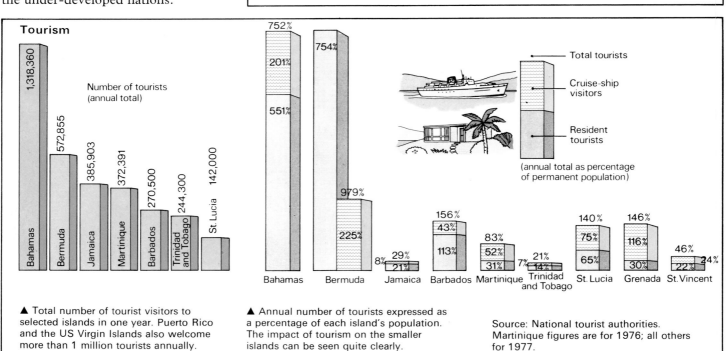

Tourism

Number of tourists (annual total)

▲ Total number of tourist visitors to selected islands in one year. Puerto Rico and the US Virgin Islands also welcome more than 1 million tourists annually.

▲ Annual number of tourists expressed as a percentage of each island's population. The impact of tourism on the smaller islands can be seen quite clearly.

Source: National tourist authorities. Martinique figures are for 1976; all others for 1977.

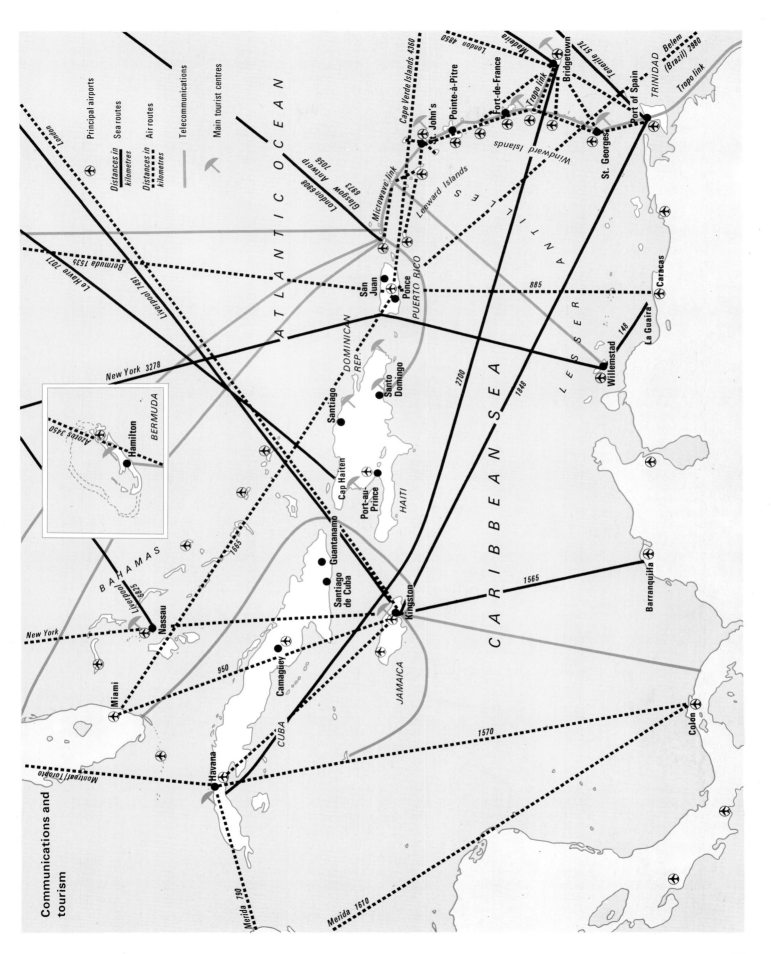

Communications and tourism

Principal airports
Sea routes
Distances in kilometres
Air routes
Distances in kilometres
Telecommunications
Main tourist centres

ATLANTIC OCEAN

London 6908
Glasgow Antwerp 7056
6973

Cape Verde Islands 4360
London 4850
Madeira
Tenerife 5176
Belem
(Brazil) 2980
Tropo link

Microwave link

St. John's
Pointe-à-Pitre
Fort-de-France
Tropo link
Bridgetown
Port of Spain
TRINIDAD

Windward Islands
St. Georges

Leeward Islands

LESSER
ANTILLES

San
Juan
Ponce
PUERTO RICO

885

Caracas

La Guaira

148

Willemstad

2700

1848

Le Havre 7011
Liverpool 7491
Bermuda 1535

New York 3278

DOMINICAN
REP.

Santiago
Santo
Domingo

CARIBBEAN SEA

Hamilton
BERMUDA
Azores 3450

Cap Haïten
Port-au-
Prince
HAITI

1565

Barranquilla

BAHAMAS

Liverpool
7435

Nassau

1665

Guantanamo
Santiago
de Cuba

Kingston

JAMAICA

New York

Miami

950

Camaguey
CUBA

Havana

1570

Colón

Montreal Toronto

Merida 790

Merida 1610

59

A brief history of the Caribbean

THE AMERINDIAN PERIOD
Communal homes built in western Caribbean. Cultivation of tobacco, sweet potato and cassava on a large scale. Skills in pottery, weaving, canoe-building and canoeing.

SPANISH COLONIZATION
1492   Spanish expedition led by Christopher Columbus lands in the Bahamas.

1494   Spanish colony of Santo Domingo founded on Hispaniola.

1508-11   Spanish begin to settle in Puerto Rico, Jamaica and Cuba.

1510   First West Africans arrive as Spanish slaves.

1515   City of Havana, Cuba, founded by Spain.

1527   Black slaves revolt in Puerto Rico

1538   University founded in Santo Domingo.

1540   English and French pirates start to raid Spanish ships and ports in the Caribbean.

THE STRUGGLE FOR LAND
1585   Francis Drake leads English raiding expedition which destroys the town of Santo Domingo.

1624   British colonies established on St. Kitts and Barbados, French colony established on St. Kitts.

1630-40   Dutch seize Curaçao, Saba, St. Maarten and St. Eustatius.

1635   French settle Guadeloupe and Martinique. Compagnie des Isles d'Amerique set up to administer French settlements.

1640-50   Dutch, French and British start to grow sugar, ending the Spanish monopoly. Land values rise steeply – up to 30 times in under ten years.

1641   Caribs drive off British forces trying to invade St. Lucia.

1655   Britain captures Jamaica from Spain.

1665   Western part of Hispaniola taken over by France as the colony of Saint-Domingue.

1671   Denmark acquires the Virgin Islands.

1688   Death of Henry Morgan, one of the last of the British pirates.

1697   Treaty of Ryswyck signed, in which Spain formally recognizes Saint-Domingue, and putting an end to piracy by the French.

1739   War in Jamaica between escaped slaves (maroons) and the authorities.

1783   Britain defeated in American War of Independence. British refugees from America flee to the Bahamas with their slaves.

1797   Britain takes over Trinidad from Spain.

REBELLION AND NATIONALISM
1804   Slaves in Saint-Domingue revolt. They defeat the French and set up the republic of Haiti.

1807   Britain stops trading in slaves.

1815   France formally recognizes British rule in Grenada, Dominica, St. Vincent, Trinidad and Tobago

1833-38   Slavery abolished in British colonies and replaced by a system of apprenticeship.

1834   Rebellion against apprenticeship system in St. Kitts.

1836   A railway is completed in Cuba – the first in Latin-America.

1844   Eastern part of Hispaniola becomes independent as the Dominican Republic.

1848   Slavery abolished in the French colonies.

1851   Cuba stops trading in slaves.

1861   Dominican Republic brought under Spanish rule following repeated invasion by Haitian troops.

1865   Rebellion put down at Morant Bay, Jamaica. Dominican Republic finally becomes independent.

1866   Oil discovered in Trinidad.

1868   War of independence begins in Cuba.

1874   Truce declared in Cuban war.

1886   Slavery finally abolished in Cuba.

1898   United States occupies Puerto Rico during Spanish-American war.

1899   United States takes over administration of Cuba.

1902   Cuba becomes independent. St. Pierre, Martinique, is destroyed when Mt. Pelée erupts, killing 40,000 people.

1917   United States buys Virgin Islands from Denmark.

1922   Imperial College of Tropical Agriculture founded in Trinidad.

1942   Large bauxite reserves confirmed in Jamaica

1944   All adults in Jamaica get the right to vote.

1946   Guadeloupe and Martinique become *départements* of France.

1952   Puerto Rico becomes an autonomous commonwealth within the United States.

1958   British colonies are combined to form the West Indies Federation

1959   Fidel Castro leads victory parade into Havana.

INDEPENDENCE AND DEVELOPMENT
1961   West Indies Federation breaks up.

1962   Jamaica becomes independent, followed by Trinidad and Tobago.

1966   Barbados becomes independent.

1973   The Bahamas become independent.

1974   Grenada become independent.

1978   Dominica becomes independent

1979   St. Lucia and St. Vincent and the Grenadines become independent.

Index